WORKING FOR CHANGE

WORKING FOR CHANGE

The movement against domestic violence

Andrew Hopkins

Heather McGregor

ALLEN & UNWIN

First published in 1991
Allen & Unwin Pty Ltd
8 Napier Street, North Sydney, NSW 2059

National Library of Australia
Cataloguing-in-Publication entry:

Hopkins, Andrew.
  Working for change
  ISBN 1 86373 019 2.

  1. Family violence — Australia. 2. Women's shelters — Australia.
  3. Abused women — Australia. I. McGregor, Heather. I. Title.
362.82920994

Set in 10/11.5 pt Times by Excel Imaging Pty Ltd, Sydney
Printed by Chong Moh Offset Printing Private Limited, Singapore

Contents

Abbreviations   vii
Acknowledgements and disclaimers   ix
Foreword   xiii
Introduction   xix

1   The women's movement and awareness of domestic violence   1
2   The refuge movement   11
3   The femocrats   27
4   The origins of the Domestic Violence Crisis Service   44
5   The crisis service as an organisational hybrid   64
6   Delivering the service   73
7   The police and the crisis service   88
8   The crisis service and the legal system   98
9   Violence in the home as crime   114
10   Strategies for social change   131

References   144

Abbreviations

DVCS	Domestic Violence Crisis Service
ALP	Australian Labor Party
DCSH	Department of Community Services and Health
OSW	Office of the Status of Women
WEL	Women's Electoral Lobby
WESP	Women's Emergency Services Program
SAAP	Supported Accommodation Assistance Program
IWY	International Women's Year
PM&C	Department of Prime Minister and Cabinet
OWA	Office of Women's Affairs
EEO	Equal Employment Opportunity
CHP	Community Health Program
DVIA	Domestic Violence Interagency
CASA	Centre Against Sexual Assault
AFP	Australian Federal Police
DPP	Director of Public Prosecutions
HEC	Hydro-electric Commission
TWS	Tasmanian Wilderness Society

Acknowledgements and disclaimers

We are grateful to the following people for their many useful comments made on earlier drafts or in interviews and discussion with us: Malise Arnstein, Glenda Blake, Dorothy Broom, Colleen Crane, David Hambly, Edna Hopkins, Lister Hopkins, Trish McDonald, Helen McKenna, Annie McLean, Jill Matthews, Jan Mundy, Lisa Paul, Nick Seddon, Dennise Simpson, Julie Roberts, Janet Ramsay, Leo Ryan, Marjanne Rook, Marian Sawer, Sue Sheridan, Chris Stanniforth, Wendy Styles, Sally Traill, Raylee Wilson, Ann Wentworth, Robyn Walmsley, Victoria Ward, Linda Webb and Julie West-Hayes. In particular we are grateful to police station commanders Don Holmes, Bill Kirk and Mal McGregor for their comments and support. We did not always take the advice of all the above people and we bear sole responsibility for the final version.

The publication of this work has been assisted by a grant from the federal Department of Community Services and Health, which expressed its support in the following terms:

> The Commonwealth Government is pleased to support the publication of this manuscript in order to promote awareness and discussion of the problems of domestic violence in Australia. This book documents the development and operation of an innovative model of domestic violence crisis support in which the Government has an interest because of its funding of a range of crisis support services under the Supported Accommodation Assistance Program. The views expressed are not necessarily those of the Commonwealth Government.

We should add that the views expressed are not necessarily those of the management committee of the Domestic Violence Crisis Service, nor of its workers. Heather McGregor does not in any sense write on behalf of the Crisis Service; nor was the book written as part of her job.

In order to ensure the confidentiality of DVCS clients, identifying details in the individual cases discussed in this book have been altered.

Many brave, daring women have made a difference to the way criminal assault at home is regarded in 1990s Australia. But the next step—stopping the violence—cannot be done by women alone. It has to be done through the action of men who are capable of acknowledging the need to recognise the rights of women. These men who do not understand as we who are women do, the everyday lives of women who are exploited, oppressed, dominated, beaten—and killed—must begin to learn through the courage of women what it means to stand out against the dominant culture. . .

All women working in the movement against violence against women are committed to eradicating it. But this must be a joint effort. Those who are not with us are against us. Those men who do not stand up in the pubs, the clubs, the workplaces, the boardrooms, the courts and the parliaments to speak out against the violence of their brothers are in favour of it. If you do not speak out with us, your silence is the voice of the complicit. The men amongst us must develop the courage of women. It is only then that the violence against which we work may be ended.

Jocelynne A. Scutt
1990

The genius of patriarchy. . . [is] compartmentalization. . .
The genius of feminist thought, culture, and action. . .[is] connectivity

Robin Morgan
1989

Foreword

Will it be believed, a hundred years hence, that such a state of things existed? (Louisa Lawson, 10 June 1891)

In the late nineteenth century Louisa Lawson railed against criminal assault at home, demanding changes to laws so that women could escape violent marriages, and calling for the establishment of refuges to which women (and the children) could run from marital cruelty, abuse and exploitation. It is indicative of the society in which we live that Louisa Lawson's writings are less well known (at least amongst those who adhere to the dominant culture) than those of her son Henry. It is also instructive that little is written of the trials of her daughter-in-law Bertha, at the violent hands of that same son, and of his failure to acknowledge his children's right to financial support. If they surface, it is generally in order to fault Bertha, and to lay at her feet a blame for Henry Lawson's alcoholism and paternal irresponsibility. (Louisa Lawson, as mother, takes the remaining blame.)

In the late twentieth century the voices may be louder, the numbers increased, but they continue to echo Louisa Lawson's words and concerns. 'Break the Silence' was a slogan created during the 1980s to signify the need for society generally to recognise and acknowledge the reality of criminal assault at home. Yet the silence was not created by the women who called for the world to listen. Women have cried out against violence in the home throughout Australia's history (at least since colonisation). The silence was imposed by the failure of those in positions of authority to hear women's voices, to hear the cries of the beaten and abused.

Working for Change documents a history of the movement against violence in the home, as that movement grew, changed, developed through the 1980s. Initially, attention was focused by the establishment of rape crisis centres around Australia, the first in Sydney in the early 1970s. Rape in marriage was defined as a crime, in limited circumstances, in South Australian law in 1976. In that same year, the Sydney Women's Electoral Lobby began drafting its Bill on Sexual Offences, which incorporated provisions making no distinction between rape as a crime inside and outside marriage. The Bill was incorporated into a Report of the Criminal Law Review Division in the New South Wales' Department of the Attorney-General and of Justice in 1978. It has since formed the basis for debate on reform of rape laws around Australia, and was central to deliberations at the National Conference on Rape Law Reform held in Hobart, Tasmania, in 1980. This appreciation of the ravages of forced sexual intercourse during marriage gave rise to an increasing public recognition of violence at home, in all its forms. In 1977 the Royal Commission on Human Relationships published its final report covering domestic violence and, amongst other matters, recommending (somewhat limitedly) that rape in marriage should be a crime where accompanied by violence, threats, false pretences or drugs and, when consent came into issue, spousal immunity should be abolished between spouses living separately and apart. In 1979 the Australian Institute of Criminology hosted the first National Conference on Violence in the Family, bringing together some 60 lawyers, refuge workers, sociologists and psychiatrists, academics, law enforcement officers and officers of various government departments and instrumentalities. Concern centred upon the background to the violence: the place of children in the family, marriage trends, and coercive parental authority; forms of violence: child abuse, child rape, sibling aggression, criminal assault at home and marital murder; the laws: reporting child abuse, apprehended domestic violence orders, rape in marriage and monetary compensation for violence in the home; and the agencies whose task it is to deal with the violence of child abuse, rape in marriage and criminal assault at home. That same year, the National Conference on Women's Advisors (to the Prime Minister and Premiers) included on its programme a paper on 'Woman Bashing: The Failure in Police Response' (Scutt, 1979).

How is it, ask Heather McGregor and Andrew Hopkins, that 'domestic' crimes of violence against women (and children) are now an agenda item in the programmes of governments around Australia? What part has been played by the women's refuge movement, by women's organisations such as the Women's Electoral Lobby, the Country Women's Association, the National Council of Jewish Women? How have women in the bureaucracy ('femocrats') worked to influence strategies devised to end violence in the home; how have they attempted to implement demands rising from the grassroots women's movement?

Andrew Hopkins and Heather McGregor centre their analysis of the 'movement against domestic violence' in the 1980s, and in a 'case study' of the development of a domestic violence crisis service in the Australian Capital Territory. Concerned to determine why Canberra should have a service which is government funded, but feminist in orientation and conception, they trace the history of women's and government's involvement in attempts to devise 'solutions'.

Canberra has often been seen as a pristine city, clinical almost in its planned roads, fenceless-but-neat homes, orderly shopping malls, row upon row of office buildings housing obedient civil servants. Violence behind the closed doors of Australia's capital? *Working for Change* answers 'yes'.

Criminal assault at home and other forms of 'domestic' violence occur with a painful regularity around Australia. Far from being immune, the Australian Capital Territory is a microcosm of the world of the bashing, beating, wrenching of arms, and pulling of hair that takes place in too many suburban, rural, outback and city homes to be dismissed as individual aberrance.

The Canberra Domestic Violence Crisis Service has been criticised for having a feminist bias, in that it seeks mainly to assist beaten women. If the world did not support battering men, there would be no women battered. Services to shore-up the emotionally injured, the physically distressed would be unnecessary were the male-biases of judicial institutions and law enforcement agencies absent. The Domestic Violence Crisis Service (and services in other states and territories) would be redundant were the entrenched ideology of 'husband-right' rendered obsolete. Yet a major sympathy of the legal system, as illustrated by *Working for Change,* is with the abuser. The reality is ignored: that the battering man has support from those very institutions women are required to call upon for help. Too often, he is within those institutions.

In 1986 Lucia Rossi, in *Give Me Strength—Forza e coraggio: Italian Australian Women Speak,* wrote of her homelife in Australia:

> At some point the ties of affection between my husband and myself were irreparably damaged. I lost my sense of humour which for many years had been my private weapon against difficulties. There was no longer love, only sullen resentment in the eyes of that companion I had sworn to love and respect 'until death'. The act of love had by then become a ritual on my husband's return from his overseas trips, as though he wanted to take possession of his woman again as he did of his bed and his favourite armchair. This hurt, and I also felt humiliated by the fact that I still desired that union. I tried to talk about this problem to the gynaecologist. Believe it or not, he read me a sermon on the insatiability of women. Every attempt to discuss the matter with my husband met with a wall of silence. What was I complaining about? I lacked nothing. I had a beautiful house, I ate well and even travelled overseas, and what would I have done with another child, since I could not even cope with two?

I tried to resign myself to the situation and look at things from his point of view. It did not even enter my head that his way of loving was nothing less than rape. Moreover, it was not just carnal violence but an attack on the soul and therefore even more shameful... (Rossi, 1989: 143)

In 1888 judges of the British House of Lords deliberated on the question whether a married woman could refuse consent to sexual intercourse with her husband. The question arose in the context of a woman being infected with syphilis or gonorrhoea by her husband. Two hundred years later, sexually-transmitted diseases remain with us; women confined to the marital bedroom yet remain vulnerable to rape. But hundreds of years of feminist lobbying has brought about fundamental change: the criminal law now rightly names rape as a crime. Around Australia, legislative change has confirmed the right of a woman to say 'no' inside as well as outside marriage. But do men listen?

Working for Change makes clear the need for affirmation additional to the written law that criminal abuses in the home are crimes. Heather McGregor and Andrew Hopkins emphasise the need for the criminal law to be *applied.* Their review of the operation of 'domestic violence orders', 'apprehension orders' or 'peace complaints' (and their equivalents in each Australian jurisdiction) makes clear the inadequacy of the 'intervention order' approach. The authors of this book believe that the existence of this mechanism is important; they see a need for the existence of laws that ostensibly provide abused women with a court order that the abusive husband desist. (They briefly outline the past and continuing debate on the 'intervention order' approach.) At the same time, they acknowledge the need for the criminality which is violence in the home to be labelled just that.

Current efforts at diversion from the criminal justice system are canvassed. To see 'counselling' or 'mediation' as a solution is, concludes *Working for Change,* wrongheaded. Counselling and mediation are designed to deal with conflict. 'Conflict' is not at the base of criminal assault at home and its violent accompanists. As Andrew Hopkins and Heather McGregor say:

One of the more common triggers to violence is a woman's failure to have the meal on the table at the prescribed time. This is a particularly revealing case because often in these circumstances there is very clearly no conflict. There is, in fact, explicit agreement, since the woman accepts that it is her duty to have his dinner ready at the appointed time and acknowledges that she has, for whatever reason, failed in her duty. The violence in these circumstances is simply punishment for non-compliance.

If, on the other hand, such a woman does not accept her partner's definition of her domestic responsibilities, there is indeed a conflict, but the violence remains a means for punishing her for denying his rules rather than a tactic for resolving conflict. Any intervention aimed at resolving the conflict over her role misses the point. The violence in this case stems from his presumed right to punish her, and it is this which must be addressed in any intervention. Unless his presumed right to punish her is challenged directly, the resolution of any particular conflict will do nothing to end the violence, because there will always be other behaviour of hers which in his view warrants punishment.

The notions of husband-right and wifely duty has a long history, and a long entrenchment in the legal system. This is readily illustrated through Family Court dispositions, as revealed in *For Richer, For Poorer—Money, Marriage and Property Rights:*

> . . .cases refer pejoratively to women's activities as duties, as if wives in performing parenting and home-making tasks are doing no more than what women are bound to do. Thus in *In the Marriage of Tranby* the court commented that 'both parties. . .[made] their appropriate contributions to the marriage, the husband by his earnings and the wife by *her duties* as parent and homemaker.' There is the subjective finding in *In the Marriage of Padstowe* that: 'I have no doubt that the wife made her contribution as parent and homemaker although *I think she lost interest in some of these duties towards the end of the period of cohabitation. . .*' A woman's 'duty' is what she 'is bound or ought to do'; those who are 'dutiful' are 'regular or willing in obedience and service'; according 'to the Oxford Dictionary 'duty' is 'behaviour due to a superior'. Should a woman suggest she should have a choice in whether or not she takes up 'her' duties full time, and under certain conditions, she runs the risk of being viewed as an incapable or inadequate performer. In *In the Marriage of Gill* the court said:
>
>> 'I am satisfied that [the husband's contributions]. . .far outweigh any contribution that may have been made by the wife as homemaker. *Her lack of interest in that calling can to an extent be gauged by her demand for "long service leave pay" or its equivalent as a condition precedent to her giving up [paid] work.'*

(Scutt and Graham, 1984: 76–7, emphasis added by S. and G.)

Yet *Working for Change* is essentially a positive book. It sees advances for women accruing in a number of ways. From the grassroots of the women's movement, demands have been noted and acted upon by government. Although the legal system must be criticised for its (lack of) performance, nonetheless some changes are discernable. Individuals within the system are, at minimum, developing an ability to listen and (hopefully) to act upon what they now hear. And the system is not monolithic: the legal system mostly advantages the powerful, but sometimes hiccups occur, and the claims of the disadvantaged gain redress.

In the end, perhaps the most positive outcomes of the movement against domestic violence have been the continuing agitation and effort of the grassroots movement, particularly the women's refuge movement; and the ability of women within government—the femocrats—to take into account the work of the women without. Certainly, differences have arisen. Disappointment has been registered by those outside about the way those inside have set their priorities. But, overall, advances have been made because women have worked, ultimately, for the good of all women. One cannot but be reminded of the words of Louisa Lawson upon the occasion of the anniversary of the feminist newspaper, *The Dawn,* in May 1889:

> . . .we pass the first white milestone on our way. For one. . .year we have travelled the uncertain path. . .[W]e gained confidence as we journeyed. For have we not met scores of women whose aims and hopes are like our own? Women whose thought-power, like that of mountain streams, is of little effect alone but which, when run into a general river of purpose, can potently aid in turning the wheel of time, to grind out a new era. (Lawson, 1990: 26)

In the 1980s Australian women added enthusiasm, professionalism and sheer hard work to the consistent effort of the women before. It provides a strong and ever strengthening base for the women of the future.

Jocelynne A. Scutt
Owen Dixon Chambers West
Melbourne, Victoria

September 1990

Introduction

Each year in Australia, perhaps a hundred women are killed and thousands are injured as a result of criminal assaults by their husbands or male partners. Children are sometimes also slain along with their mothers when men massacre their entire family, as happened in Canberra and Brisbane as this book was going to press. Apart from the women who are killed or injured, countless more live in fear for their lives. This book is about the movement against such violence and the processes leading to the emergence of the movement.

While there have always been men who beat their wives, the contemporary movement against domestic violence goes back only to the 1970s. The first feminist refuge for victims of violence in Australia was established in 1974 in Sydney. Interestingly, the 'discovery' of the problem of wife beating had taken place almost contemporaneously in the USA, where the first women's shelter was established in the same year, and in the UK, where the first shelter started operation in 1971. In Australia the number of women's refuges grew rapidly, but it was only in the 1980s that the problem of domestic violence began to receive wider attention. Various law reform commissions and government task forces have reported on the matter and, starting with New South Wales in 1982, every state and territory in Australia has now enacted new domestic violence legislation.

In late 1979 the Australian Institute of Criminology held the first national conference on 'violence in the family'. This event was repeated on a much larger scale in 1985, this time as a conference on 'domestic violence'. This second conference, held at the request of the Attorney-General and attended by over 300 participants, was said to be the largest and most demanding ever conducted by the Institute (Hatty, 1986: iii). Academics in Australia also turned their attention to the subject, among the best known results being a book by feminist lawyer Jocelynne Scutt, *Even in the Best of Homes,* published in 1983.

During the 1980s women's units in various state governments have run publicity campaigns against violence in the home, and in 1987 the Office of the Status of Women in the Department of

Prime Minister and Cabinet set in motion a research programme which included a major survey of community attitudes to domestic violence. This revealed a disquieting level of community tolerance of violence by men against their wives. Accordingly, the federal government began a campaign to change community attitudes, the high point of which was National Domestic Violence Awareness Month in April, 1989. The month was publicly launched by the Prime Minister and featured a major series of television advertisements. The campaign ran for three years, with an annual budget of close to a million dollars.

It is clear, then, that a movement against domestic violence has developed in recent years in Australia, as it has in other countries (Studer, 1984: 415). It is clear, too, that the movement is an outgrowth of feminism. Critics who say that the women's movement has lost momentum would do well to consider the impact that feminism continues to have in this area.

It is quite striking, however, that domestic violence was *not* one of the initial concerns of the women's movement which arose in Australia at the end of the 1960s; it emerged as an issue only in the mid-1970s. Chapter 1 explores the reasons for this delay and argues that it was primarily an outcome of the initial focus of the women's movement on discrimination in public life, where male violence was not an issue.

Two strands of feminism have been particularly influential in promoting concern about domestic violence: the refuge movement, and the 'femocrats'—feminist bureaucrats in government. Chapter 2 is devoted to the refuge movement and analyses its twin concerns: to provide emergency housing for battered women and to work against domestic violence. At times the housing question swamped the social change concerns but in the long run the refuges became an important source of the broader movement against domestic violence. The chapter describes the refuges' fight for funding. It also discusses the 'feminist collective' as an organisational form and shows how this both contributes to refuge goals and creates difficulties for bureaucrats who deal with the refuges.

Feminist bureaucrats (femocrats) have been an important feature of the women's movement in Australia. Their relationship to the broader movement has been much debated in recent years (Franzway et al. 1989; Yeatman, 1990) and the present work can be seen as a contribution to that debate. Chapter 3 deals first with the general debate. It then considers the femocrat role and shows that this varies considerably, depending on the issue. On some matters femocrats take the initiative, acting independently of the wider movement and even unrecognised by it, while on other issues the impetus comes from the wider movement with femocrats acting in a sense as the movement's agents within government. In relation to the funding of refuges, femocrats have been the agents of the movement. Likewise, the present federal government campaign is a response to suggestions from the broader movement. However, in the case of the present campaign, a femocrat initiative, the National Agenda for Women, was vital in enabling the broader movement to express itself the way it has.

In analysing the contribution of the two groups to the movement against domestic violence, our conclusion is that refuge workers were the main driving force and that the activities of femocrats have been vitally important in enabling the movement to gather momentum. It is essentially the collaboration between these two groups which has enabled the movement to make the progress it has.

One of the milestones in the progress of the movement has been the establishment in Canberra of a Domestic Violence Crisis Service (DVCS). The DVCS is a true crisis intervention service. It is staffed 24 hours a day, seven days a week by teams of workers, equipped with cars and mobile phones, prepared to attend in any crisis situation to assist the victim, provided the police are also in attendance to prevent further violence and provided there is an invitation from some member of the household. Thus, although a totally independent service, it works in close collaboration with the police. DVCS workers are also available to take victims to court following an episode of violence, to seek a domestic violence order, restraining the perpetrator from further violence. Many of these orders involve the eviction of the man from the house, something almost unheard of elsewhere in Australia.

The service is the first of its kind in Australia. Some states have domestic violence telephone counselling services while others have crisis intervention services which operate less than 24 hours a day. There are also various police units specialising in domestic violence. The only other 24-hour-a-day crisis intervention service in Australia to date, Adelaide's Crisis Care Unit, established in 1976, is not specifically concerned with domestic violence although it does handle such cases. Most importantly, the DVCS is the onlynon-governmental service and the only service with an explicit feminist ideology.

Chapter 4 recounts the history of the establishment of this service. It discusses the processes of law reform in the early 1980s and shows how these gave rise to a suggestion for a crisis intervention service. It describes how refuge workers and femocrats then joined forces to push for and eventually achieve a service with a feminist ideology built into its very constitution. In the case of the establishment of the DVCS in Canberra, input from both groups was vital and it was the partnership between the two which determined the outcome.

Although a feminist service, the DVCS was set up not as a feminist collective but as a hierarchy, with clear lines of accountability. However, it was initially largely staffed by ex-refuge workers, accustomed to working in collectives. This has had interesting organisational consequences which are addressed in chapter 5. We describe the DVCS as having a 'hybrid organisational form', part collective and part hierarchy, and we argue that such a form is particularly appropriate for organisations seeking the type of social change pursued by the movement against domestic violence.

The attitudes of the police and the courts, which are simply a reflection of widely held community views, make it very difficult for victims of assault in the home to obtain justice or protection from the legal system. Chapters 6, 7 and 8 recount the experiences of the DVCS in supporting the victims of violence and in dealing with the police and the legal system. Because of its feminist philosophy, the service has encountered considerable misunderstanding and sometimes hostility, but is slowly winning acceptance. The DVCS has played a significant role in educating police and other legal system personnel about the criminal nature of 'domestics' and in helping women to use the legal system to maximum advantage. It has thus become an agent of social change in its own right.

The movement against domestic violence raises a number of more general questions which we address in the latter part of the book. Chapter 9 raises the question of whether it is really appropriate to treat violence in the home as criminal and punishable. A possible alternative is to see domestic violence as an expression of conflict between the parties requiring interventions aimed at conflict resolution rather than punishment. We argue that, contrary to a view widely held in criminological circles, the criminal law can bring about behavioural changes for certain types of crime and that wife bashing is a case in point. We argue, too, that it is only by the systematic use of the criminal law in this area that we can hope to bring about real changes in community attitudes to domestic violence.

Chapter 10 discusses in a more general way the sources of social change. Unlike the environment movement, for example, which has developed because of the increasing threat to the environment, the movement against domestic violence is not a response to any increase in the level of wife beating; there is certainly no evidence of any such increase. Instead, it is a product of feminist ideology and, as such, testimony to the power of ideas. This would seem to confound the more pessimistic view of certain social scientists that social change depends upon changes in material circumstances. It suggests that human beings are not simply the passive products of their society but can make choices to bring about changes in that society.

A question of theoretical interest and practical importance which confronts those seeking social change is whether, on the one hand, to focus on grassroots action, that is, changing or helping people at the individual level, or on the other, to seek to persuade governments to implement legislative or administrative changes. This is a debate which besets most movements for social change and which is very much an issue for those working against domestic violence. Our analysis is designed to cast light on this question.

In this book we have chosen to use the terms 'domestic violence' and 'wife or woman bashing' interchangeably. We do not believe we are guilty of significant gender bias in so doing. It is true that studies have shown that women sometimes hit their husbands. But these male 'victims' are rarely in fear of their lives and rarely unable to protect themselves. Men are seldom injured in such episodes. In almost every 'domestic' to which the police are summoned it is a woman who is the victim. It is also true that women sometimes murder their husbands. Indeed in the great majority of killings by women, the victim is the husband (Queensland Task Force, 1988: 152). But such murders are almost always a desperate final response to years of being beaten and/or to incest perpetrated by the husband on the children (Queensland Task Force, 1988: 15). We do not, however, address these mattters in detail in the book. The fact is that the movement against domestic violence is concerned with violence against women in the home. In writing about this movement, then, we are writing about a movement against male, not female, violence.

Recently, there has been a move to refer to victims of violence as 'survivors'. These women are indeed survivors of dreadful adversity. The rationale for this move is that the word 'victim' has a negative meaning in some circles and the phrase 'behaving like a victim' is used disparagingly. We have come hesitantly to the view, however, that the term 'survivor' is somewhat of a euphemism. It tends to divert attention away from the fact that the woman is indeed the victim of a criminal assault. Furthermore the view that a beaten woman is surviving may actually reinforce the idea that the violence is not all that serious. What is important is to relate to a victim's resourcefulness respectfully and not to deny the seriousness of what is happening to her. It is largely for these reasons that we have chosen in this book to refer to women who are damaged physically or psychologically by the behaviour of their male part-ners, with the greatest respect, as 'victims'.

Our interest in the movement against domestic violence stems from our professional activities. Heather McGregor was the first coordinator of the DVCS and now directs the section on Violence Against Women and Legal Matters in the federal government's Office of the Status of Women. For many years prior to these appointments she worked as a relationship counsellor and as an educator in the fields of human relations and behavioural health. Andrew Hopkins is a sociologist and criminologist at the Austra-lian National University who teaches courses dealing with move-ments for social change and with the sociology of law and white-collar crime. This book is a joint and equal effort.

1 The women's movement and awareness of domestic violence

A first wave of feminism developed in Australia in the late nineteenth century, aimed primarily at achieving the vote for women (Sawer and Simms, 1984). Its very success in this respect was one the factors leading to its decline in the early twentieth century. It is noteworthy, though, that domestic violence was one of the matters about which these early feminists protested vehemently (Hatty, 1987: 6). The present wave of Australian feminism emerged around 1970. This is not to say that feminists were not active in the intervening period; they were, as has recently been documented (Daniels and Murnane, 1989). But there was undoubtedly a resurgence at the end of the 1960s. In this chapter we shall explore, in a preliminary way, the relationship between this second wave and the growth of the movement against domestic violence. In later chapters we shall continue this exploration by considering, more specifically, the refuge movement and the role of feminists in the bureaucracy.

At first sight the connection between feminism and the growth of concern about domestic violence seems so obvious as to need no explanation. But the intriguing fact is that the current movement against domestic violence in Australia gathered momentum only in the 1980s, more than a decade after the women's movement itself emerged. Why this should be so is the puzzle which motivates this chapter. To begin with, we need to go back to the origins of contemporary feminism in Australia.

The women's liberation movement, as it was originally, grew out of the new-left politics of the 1960s (Curthoys, 1984; Dixson, 1986; Sawer and Simms, 1984). On the campuses, in particular, this was a time of protest against the Vietnam War, of support for the liberation struggles of the Vietnamese and other oppressed groups and of renewal of the socialist vision. The new left differed from the old in that it was largely a middle-class movement, which, furthermore, did not see its fate as tied in any way to the fortunes of the Soviet Union. Indeed, it identified with the uprising of the Czechs against Soviet occupying forces in Prague in 1968. Organisationally, it rejected the more disciplined party structures of the old left in favour of anarchist ideas and a commitment to a thoroughgoing participatory democracy.

Women were very much a part of the new politics, but they found that they were relegated by their male counterparts to support roles, such as making the coffee at meetings. This they resented. As Curthoys puts it: 'new left men who had been so concerned about the fate of the Vietnamese had been happily dominating, denigrating, and exploiting new left women, and those women had finally had enough' (1984: 162). The women's liberation movement began, then, as a revolt by new-left women against their oppression by new-left men. Its very first action in Sydney was to distribute a pamphlet, 'only the chains have changed', at an anti-war demonstration in December 1969 (Wills, 1983: 322).

Given their initial concerns, it is not surprising that many of the early women's liberationists saw the oppression of women as somehow secondary to the more fundamental inequalities of class. Blaikie (cited in Sawer and Simms, 1984: 176) recalls that the women of the Monash University Labour Club accepted the view of male club members that their primary commitment had to be to working-class revolution and that women's liberation should not be allowed to divert them from this aim. They even argued at the first Women's Liberation Conference in Melbourne in 1970 that men should be admitted to the conference. For these women, the liberation of women was little more than the means to a greater goal, the liberation of the working class.

It may seem ironic that the women's movement in Australia had its origins in a struggle against a quite different form of oppression. Yet this seems to have been the experience of the women's movement in other countries, as well. In particular, the development of feminism in many third-world countries was stimulated by struggles against military dictatorships. Nicaragua, where the Somoza dictatorship was overthrown by the Sandinista National Liberation Front in 1979, is a case in point. A national organisation of women was first formed just two years prior to the final defeat of Somoza and was named, revealingly, 'The Assocation of Women Confronting the National Question', that is, the dictatorship. Furthermore, women took an active part in fighting. A celebrated raid on the national assembly, in which legislators were taken hostage and then released in exchange for a number of gaoled Sandinista leaders, was led by a woman commandant. That women could have made such advances in a Latin American country with a traditional macho culture is little short of astonishing.

The explanation is provided by the women themselves (Randall, 1980). Oppressed in all the ways that their menfolk were, and in addition subjected on a daily basis to rape and other sexual abuse by the troops of Somoza's national guard, they were eager to join the Sandinista Front and take to the hills for the fight against the dictator. However, they found themselves thwarted in this desire. Husbands would often seek to prevent them from participating, and in the field they were often relegated by their male companions to essentially domestic tasks: looking after the fighting men, carrying messages, and organising safe houses. They rapidly realised that if they were really to take part in the armed struggle against Somoza they would first have to tackle the macho assumptions of their male comrades. Thus the feminist battle went hand in hand with the battle against Somoza.

Of course, to return to the Australian case, the concerns of new-left women were not the only factor accounting for the re-emergence of the women's movement at the beginning of the 1970s. Other, more impersonal forces were at work. More women were entering higher education and, in the 1960s, 'the pill' was facilitating changes in sexual behaviour and greater control over reproduction. Moreover, the numbers of women in paid employment were steadily increasing. The table below shows the growth in the employment of women since the Second World War, the figures being particularly striking in the case of married women. In the decade most relevant to our discussion, 1961 to 1971, the percentage of all women in the workforce rose from 29 to 37 per cent, while for married women it leapt from 17 to 33 per cent.

Percentage of women in the Australian labour force

Year	Married women	All women
1947	6.5	24.9
1954	12.6	26.3
1961	17.3	28.9
1966	26.6	35.2
1971	32.8	37.1
1976	43.8	43.8
1981	42.3	44.6

Source: Eccles, 1984: 81

These changes were of profound importance. The influx of educated women in particular into the workforce was a key factor underpinning second-wave feminism. As Curthoys puts it: 'the social base of modern feminism was the expanding group of women who were entering the professional, technical, administrative and skilled occupations' (1984: 163). For these middle-class women, the disadvantages they experience are associated with gender and not class. For this reason the women's liberation movement rapidly disentangled itself from the class concerns of its founders and began to attract adherents who had no interest in socialist or left-wing politics (Curthoys, 1984: 164).

A further factor which influenced the movement's timing in Australia was its emergence in the USA in the 1960s. Betty Friedan's best selling book, *The Feminine Mystique*, appeared in the USA in 1963, and the National Organization of Women (NOW) was formed in 1966. Self-identified women's liberation groups began forming from about 1967, interestingly, among new-left women reacting to the sexism of new-left men (Freeman, 1983: 17–21). These developments did not go unnoticed in Australia.

THE EARLY AGENDA

What, then, were the issues which concerned the women's movement in the early phase? According to Curthoys, who has written one of the most detailed histories to date, the demands of the new women's movement 'included equal pay, free 24-hour childcare, work opportunities, the right to abortion' (1984: 165). Elsewhere she writes, 'the key issues were housework, childcare, work opportunities, pay, abortion, and sexual exploitation and objectification' (1984: 164). Elizabeth Reid, the first women's advisor to the Prime Minister, recalls that in the early 1970s 'most of us in the movement had been associated with single issue reform groups: abortion, homosexuality, equal pay'. At the legislative level, she writes, the following changes were to be sought: 'equal pay, retraining, childcare, part-time employment, control over our health' (1987: 12). In her history of Sydney women's liberation Wills notes that 'during these early years the two major campaigns of the movement's activities were around the issues of abortion and work' (1983: 315). Finally, Dowse observes that the campaign by the Women's Electoral Lobby in 1972 'was based upon the six demands formulated by women's liberation: equal pay, equal employment opportunity, equal opportunity in education, free contraceptive services, abortion on demand and free, 24-hour childcare' (1983: 204).

From the present point of view what is most significant about these lists of priorities is that none of them includes domestic violence. Also conspicuously absent is the question of rape. In fact the whole issue of male violence, of such central concern to feminists a few years later, was simply not on the agenda at the beginning of the 1970s.

In seeking to understand why, let us first characterise the demands which *were* on the agenda. These were of two kinds: demands concerning reproduction and childcare, and demands for an end to discrimination against women in the public sphere, particularly the workplace. The first set of concerns arose from the realisation that the traditional women's role of bearing and raising children was one of the principal factors impeding the full participation of women in public life, especially in the paid workforce. Given the central role of paid employment in this society, not only in providing access to material resources but also in the maintenance of self-esteem, it is easy to understand why the demands for ready access to birth control and abortion and for free childcare services assumed such importance for the women's movement from the outset.

The other set of demands concerned the provision of equal opportunity in the workplace and the removal of all forms of discrimination. It seems incredible now that married women were barred from permanent employment in the Australian public service until 1966; prior to that time a woman who married was required to resign! Moreover, women in Australia had traditionally received lower wages than men for the same work. During the 1960s pressure for the removal of this form of discrimination developed and from 1969 to 1974 a series of decisions by the Arbitration Commission facilitated progress towards the goal of equal pay for work of equal value (Nieuwenhuysen and Hicks, 1975: 76–81). Many other forms of discrimination, less blatant perhaps but equally detrimental to women, fuelled the demands for equal opportunity.

What these demands all have in common is that they do not focus on the behaviour of men, but rather on the activities of the state. They are demands that the *state* provide free childcare, that the *state* legislate to end its own discrimination and that of other employers in the workplace, and so on. They are not addressed to men and do not, in the first instance, seek change in the behaviour of individual men. They are notably silent about the relationships between men and women in the domestic sphere. This is a particularly striking omission, given that most present-day accounts locate the origins of gender inequality in the domestic arena: in the domestic division of labour and in the patriarchal relations which exist between husband and wife. In terms of the distinction so often made between the public and private spheres of life, the demands of the early women's liberationists were aimed very much at public life.

The preceding point is vividly illustrated by the childcare issue. If women are disadvantaged by their traditional childcare role, there are at least two ways of rectifying the problem. One is to demand that the state provide free childcare, to enable women to go out to work or to pursue other activities. This is a demand that the state shoulder some of the responsibility for childcare; it leaves the role of men unchanged. An alternative is to demand that men share the responsibility for childcare. This involves changes in the private relationships of men and women and a shift in the balance of power and responsibility in domestic life. Such demands were not initially on the agenda.

EXPLAINING THE AGENDA

Clearly, if the spotlight was on public life, domestic violence could not come into focus. But we have yet to explore the reasons for this public gaze. A first and perhaps obvious point is that it is, in principle, much easier to bring about changes in the public arena than in the private. Equal pay for equal work could be brought about by decisions of the Conciliation and Arbitration Commission; abortion on demand, free childcare and so on require only a decision by government. Of course such policy changes may necessitate long political battles, which in many cases have not yet been won, but the point is that once the policy decision has been made, substantial changes follow.

Change in the private sphere is altogether more difficult to achieve. What is needed here is value change and changes in the dynamics of personal relationships. This involves challenging the very essence of patriarchy, and not just the modification of some of its, arguably, more peripheral manifestations. Such changes cannot be readily brought about by legislation, although legislation does have its part to play, as we shall argue later. They depend, rather, upon the whole range of projects on which the women's movement is now engaged and which may take generations to show results.

Dowse (1984: 142) points out another reason, perhaps peculiar to Australia, why feminists looked to the state from the outset to solve their problems. It is an Australian tradition. The early white Australians were not free settlers but employees of the British Crown, and their charges. The state was, from the beginning, an inescapable presence. As the nineteenth century progressed, governments remained an all-pervasive fact of life, taking on a variety of welfare functions, and it seemed natural for the individual to rely on the state to protect his or her interests. As Sir Keith Hanncock wrote earlier this century, 'to the Australian, the State means collective power at the service of individualistic rights' (cited in Dowse, 1984: 142). Dowse, a former head of the Office of Women's Affairs, sees herself as influenced by this tradition: 'My expectations are low, but my directions are clear. I look to the public sector. And despite all claims to the contrary, so do most of my feminist sisters, even the most radical among them' (1984: 139).

The conceptual framework in terms of which the position of women was understood in those first years also encouraged a focus on public life. In the absence of any better way of looking at it, the problem was seen as one of discrimination and the predicament of women rapidly began to be seen as analogous to the situation of oppressed racial minorities, particularly the blacks in the USA. Indeed, although constituting more than half the population, women were often described as a minority group. That the logical absurdity of this description was simply ignored is testimony to the hold which the race analogy had on thinking at the time.

For it was a useful analogy. The very word 'sexism' was coined by analogy with 'racism'. It brought into play the rhetoric of the American civil rights movement of the 1960s and highlighted the discrimination which women experienced in public life. Indeed, the sit-ins in public bars in Australia, in protest against the refusal of hotels to serve women, were highly reminiscent of the campaigns by blacks in the USA a few years earlier to desegregate 'whites only' facilities.

But it was also a severely limited analogy. What blacks were demanding was equal treatment before the law and an end to discrimination in public life. The prejudices which whites might privately harbour against blacks were of secondary importance, provided they did not adversely affect the opportunities of blacks in public life. What did it matter if a white man did not want his daughter to marry one, assuming for the sake of the argument that she shared his prejudice? After all, blacks might prefer to marry blacks. Marital choices based on skin colour, religion or any other criterion are a matter for the individual and cannot reasonably be objected to by others; it is only when such prejudices spill over into public life that they become oppressive. This line of thinking has led some groups campaigning against racism in the workplace to abandon any attempt to change racist attitudes and to focus exclusively on racist workplace practices. The assumption is that once the practices are changed the attitudes will fall into line, or at least lose much of their significance (Chambers and Pettman, 1986).

None of this is true for the oppression of women. The removal of discrimination in public life is only one aspect of women's liberation. Patriarchy expresses itself most fundamentally in the home and it is here that the struggle for the liberation of women must ultimately take place. The race analogy, with its focus on discrimination, ignored the critical domestic aspect of patriarchal relations, and in so doing, tended to retard the growth of awareness of violence in the home.

THE CONSPIRACY OF SILENCE

Another reason the women's movement did not concern itself with domestic violence from the very outset is that the problem was essentially hidden from view. There is, as many writers have observed, a conspiracy of silence when it comes to questions of male violence in the home. The conspiracy involves both the victims of violence and the authorities who might be in a position to do something about it. Their reasons, however, are quite distinct. Police, medical authorites and others who come into contact with domestic violence or its consequences in the course of their work, have traditionally ignored it as far as possible, largely on the grounds that it is a private matter between a husband and his wife, in which outsiders have little right to interfere. This attitude is based on the belief that a man's home is his castle and should be inviolable; the fact that it may also be a woman's home is overlooked.

Women participate in this conspiracy out of guilt, shame and fear. Victims of violence are usually brainwashed by perpetrators into believing that they are in some way responsible for the violence—that it is their fault. They are ashamed to acknowledge what is happening, believing that their experience is not shared by others, and they are often fearful that, should they complain, the violence might escalate. Hence they remain in their own private hell, unable to see the broad pattern of injustice of which they are victims.

Domestic violence could only move onto the agenda when its victims began to speak up, and this could only happen after the movement had begun to have an effect on women's thinking. Vital to this development was the strategy of 'consciousness raising'. Quite apart from issue-oriented protest groups, an important feature of the movement from the outset was the proliferation of small discussion groups aimed at examining the personal experience of participants and raising awareness of the collective nature of privately experienced pain (Sawer and Simms, 1984: 1784). It is in this context that the feminist slogan—'the personal is political'—takes on such significance, for once women began to realise that their personal experiences were part of a wider pattern, these experiences could be formulated as political issues and take their place on the feminist agenda.

It seems, from accounts by those involved at the time, that the publication of a particular book in 1974 also played a part in bringing domestic violence out into the open. *Scream Quietly or the Neighbours Will Hear* described Erin Pizzey's experiences in setting up a women's refuge in Britain in 1971, and it is no coincidence that the first women's refuges in Australia and in the USA were established immediately following the appearance of this publication.

FOCUSING ON MALE VIOLENCE

It was not until the mid-1970s that feminist theory began to give real prominence to questions of male violence. The early analogy with racism started to give way to the concept of patriarchy from 1970 onwards, following the publication of Kate Millett's *Sexual Politics*. This book, which according to Curthoys was received by the women's moment in Australia with great excitement, defined patriarchy as a governing ideology and a set of institutions, such as the family, work and the state, which functioned in the interests of men. Millet did not highlight the issue of male violence, because she did not regard force as the principal technique of patriarchal control in modern societies. In the mid-1970s, however, the theoretical ground shifted again, with the publication of two influential books dealing centrally with male violence: Brownmiller's (1975) and Daly's (1978). Perhaps the most famous proposition in this new theoretical armoury was Brownmiller's claim that rape 'is nothing more nor less than a conscious process by which *all men* keep *all women* in a state of fear'. Here at last was a set of ideas which might swing the spotlight onto domestic violence.

In a general way, the agenda of women's liberation in Australia moved in tandem with these changing theoretical formulations. Wills (1983) has provided us with a detailed chronology of the movement's activities in Sydney. The first mention of any activity prompted by male violence occurs in 1974 with a forum on Women against the Violent Society. In the same year Australia's first refuge for victims of domestic violence was opened, as was Sydney's Rape Crisis Centre. Other activities directed at male violence followed, perhaps the most publicised being the attempts in the late 1970s to lay wreaths on Anzac Day in memory of all women raped in war. According to Curthoys (1984: 172), from about the mid-1970s probably more women in the movement were concerned about questions of male violence, especially rape, domestic violence and pornography than with questions of discrimination in the world of work.

A particular aspect of this emphasis on male violence was the work by various groups of women in the mid and late 1970s to reform rape laws to include the possibility of prosecution for rape within marriage. Naturally, public discussion of the issue of rape in marriage reinforced concerns about domestic violence more generally. As Scutt puts it in her foreword to this book: 'this appreciation of the ravages of forced sexual intercourse during marriage gave rise to an increasing public recognition of violence in the home in all its forms'.

CONCLUSION

The question with which we began this chapter was why it was that widespread public concern about domestic violence developed only in the 1980s, more than a decade after the contemporary wave of Australian feminism began to roll. This chapter goes some way to providing an answer. Domestic violence was simply not one of the concerns which triggered the emergence of the movement. The intital focus was on various forms of gender discrimination which those first women's liberationists saw as impeding their full and equal participation in public life. Moreover, the ideological tools to hand, in particular the race analogy, tended to blinker the gaze of the movement, directing it away from the domestic sphere and certainly away from male violence. It was only with the theoretical developments of the mid-1970s that such issues could come clearly into focus. Finally, the conspiracy of silence which surrounds domestic violence made it difficult for the issue to emerge until the movement had reached a certain level of visibility and maturity.

Once formulated as an issue, two distinct strands of the women's movement played a role in making domestic violence the matter of public concern it is today: the refuge movement, and feminists working in government bureaucracies—the femocrats. We take up these strands in succeeding chapters.

2   The refuge movement

The women's refuge movement emerged suddenly in the mid-1970s. In March 1974 a group of Sydney feminists, defying the law, squatted in a couple of tiny derelict houses in Glebe and offered accommodation to battered women and their children (Girdler, 1982: 152). They were immediately inundated by women, prepared to live in overcrowded and sub-standard conditions, in order to get away from violence (Johnson, 1981: vii). So began Elsie, Australia's first feminist refuge. A group of Melbourne women had simultaneously been discussing the possiblity of setting up a refuge and two of them travelled to Sydney to be present when the houses in Glebe were occupied. Soon afterwards a Melbourne woman donated a rent-free house in the suburb of Kew, and it became Melbourne's first refuge, known simply as the 'half-way house' (*The Age,* 5 January 1990, p. 8).

The new Sydney refuge clearly caught the imagination of people all over the country, for when the Australian Labor Party (ALP), concerned about its re-election prospects, conducted a survey of what women wanted, it found that refuges were high on the list of priorities (McFerren, 1987: 30). And so, when Elsie applied to the federal government for funding, the response was sympathetic. Within a year of the events in Glebe, eleven refuges were either in operation or about to open their doors, and in mid-1975 the federal government announced funding for them all (Dowse 1984: 148–9). By 1979, just five years after Elsie's opening, there were 93 women's refuges receiving federal funding and an estimated 100 in operation (Dowse, 1984: 149). About half of these were run by women's groups, the remainder being largely church run (Australian Housing Research Council, 1980: 43). By 1987 the federal government was funding 163 women's refuges and a further 20 non-accommodation support services (Ford, 1988: 10,13).

The number of people assisted by the refuges throughout Australia is quite staggering. In 1989 there were approximately 2500 people in women's refuges on any one day, slightly more than half of them children (unpublished data from Department of Community Services and Health). Figures for 1984 reveal that approximately 31 000 women and children passed through the refuges in that year (Office of the Status of Women (OSW) data). Clearly, the establishment of Elsie started a chain reaction which, fuelled by the previously unacknowledged plight of large numbers of battered women in the community, resulted in the explosive growth of refuges around the country.

The proportion of refuges run by feminist groups has tended to decline. However, estimates of the numbers involved are difficult to obtain. According to one source, in 1984 only one of Queensland's 22 refuges was explicitly feminist (Smith, 1985: 33). On the other hand, in Victoria the majority of the currently funded refuges are said by federal government sources to be feminist, while in the ACT, four of the five women's refuges are feminist. Be this as it may, it was the feminist refuges which set the whole process in motion and which were most visible in the fight for funding. It is also the feminist refuges which have been most self-consciously and deliberately part of the movement against domestic violence. For these reasons, they are the focus of this chapter.

This perspective explains why we have chosen to begin our account of the refuge movement with the establishment of the Sydney refuge in 1974, rather than with the Warrawee refuge in Fremantle, described in one account as the first women's refuge (Australian Housing Research Council, 1980). The Warrawee shelter was set up by the Fremantle Council in 1971. It was not motivated by a concern about domestic violence but by a shortage of temporary accommodation for women and children. As documentation at the time argued: 'there are a number of boarding and rooming houses in Fremantle which cater for men only, but none for women and children'. Warrawee was known when it opened as an 'occasional accommodation centre'. It was not until the refuge movement got under way in the eastern states that it developed into a feminist refuge. In short, the establishment of Warrawee was an isolated event, not strictly a part of the refuge movement we have described.

WHAT IS A REFUGE?

Refuges are often large suburban houses which can only be identified by the high fence which surrounds some of them. Most have a restricted entrance through a reception area or office. Men are not allowed in most refuges, and staff will not give information about a resident to outsiders without her permission.

Refuge staff, almost always women, are on duty 24 hours a day to provide assistance and protection. Women can come to the refuge at any time of the day or night. . .Most only stay a few nights or weeks. . .

Inside the refuge the atmosphere is as close to an ordinary home as possible. Families have their own bedroom or may have to share with another family. (This is a major source of tension in refuges and many now limit numbers to ensure only one family per room.) Other areas of the house are shared. Residents are encouraged to mix with and support each other. Residents share the housework.

All refuges charge a small contribution, though it is often waived if a family has no money. Some refuges provide food with meals communally cooked; in others, residents buy and cook for themselves. Bedding, and in some refuges basic toiletries, are provided. Also clothes and emergency money for families who left home without their belongings.

Most refuges have large yards or gardens, with separate play areas and staff for children. School-aged children are encouraged to attend the local school . . .

Women are free to come and go as they please, and in some refuges they can leave their children with child-care workers if they have an appointment or other business. (McFerren, 1987: 45)

THE REFUGE MOVEMENT IN CONTEXT

Before describing the evolution of the refuges in greater detail, it is worth locating this new development in the context of the wider women's movement. Historians of the women's movement in Australia frequently divide it into two wings: women's liberation and WEL, the Women's Electoral Lobby (Sawer and Simms, 1984; Wills, 1983). The term 'women's liberation', widely used in the early days of the movement, has largely disappeared, but the phenomenon itself hasn't. According to this analysis, the women's liberation movement is a grassroots phenomenon: a large number of autonomous and uncoordinated groups, concerned with a variety of issues, emphasising solidarity and consciousness raising and lacking spokeswomen. This was really all there was to the women's movement until 1972, when the WEL was formed, specifically to play a part in the federal election of that year. WEL was nationally organised, carefully structured, with a constitution, annual conferences and official spokeswomen. It did not, however, have a hierarchical structure or elected officials. Its first task was to interrogate election candidates on their attitudes to a variety of women's issues and to publicise the results, in an effort to get politicians sympathetic to women's concerns elected. Thereafter, WEL has systematically lobbied governments at state and federal levels, seeking to have policies beneficial to women adopted.

A recent analysis of WEL (Sawer, 1990) suggests that the distinction traditionally drawn between the organisational styles of WEL and women's liberation may have been overdrawn, WEL being rather more decentralised and grassroots in its orientation than this analysis would suggest. But a distinction there is. Furthermore, in terms of this analysis, the refuge movement is, on the whole, an outgrowth of the grassroots or women's liberation wing of feminism. Again, this observation needs qualification: in certain cases, for example in Canberra, WEL women were very much involved in the establishment of refuges.

Writers who distinguish between WEL and women's liberation usually characterise the politics of the two wings as respectively reformist and radical. WEL epitomises a liberal feminist tradition which is happy to work within the existing framework to achieve reforms. This tradition assumes that neither the state nor the existing social structure is *inherently* patriarchal. On this view, gender equality can be achieved by a series of piecemeal reforms, without the need for fundamental or revolutionary change.

Women's liberation, on the other hand, favours a more revolutionary line. According to this view, the existing structures are inherently patriarchal and there is little point in working with or through them. Real change can come about only by working at the grassroots level to empower women directly. Hence an emphasis on refuges, rape crisis services, consciousness raising and collective forms of organisation. As Sawer and Simms put it, women's liberation aims to change the nature of the economic and social pie while WEL aims simply to provide women with a more generous serve of the existing pie (1984: 186).

Women's liberationists have been divided further into socialist and so-called radical feminists. (Sawer and Simms, 1984: 192). The former see the oppression of women as related in various ways to the oppression of the working class and stress the need to be sensitive to class divisions within the women's movement which have the potential to fragment it. The latter see the problem more simply as one of patriarchy, from which all women suffer equally. The division surfaced in a dramatic way at the International Women's Conference in Mexico in 1975, held to mark the beginning of the United Nations decade for women (Barrios, 1978). Various impoverished third-world women described the appalling conditions in which they and their husbands worked on the plantations and in the mines, and argued that the primary source of their oppression was class, not gender. They resented the argument of radical first-world feminists at the conference that they should put aside these concerns and condemn their own menfolk as the fundamental source of their oppression. A similar issue threatened to divide the Women and Politics conference held in Canberra in 1975, when black women argued that the radical feminist line overlooked the racial exploitation from which they and their black brothers suffered. However, according to Sawer and Simms (1984: 192), the distinction between radical and socialist feminism tends to break down in practice and is of little significance in the day-to-day politics of women's liberation.

We are left, on this analysis, with a broad division of the women's movement into two wings, one seeking reform and the other revolution. And the refuge movement, from this point of view, is located at the revolutionary end of the political spectrum.

But this is an unhappy formulation. It has often been pointed out that the distinction between reform and revolution is by no means absolute. A series of reforms may over time amount to a revolution, while so-called revolutions sometimes fail to bring about fundamental changes in the societies in which they occur. As for the refuge movement, although often seen as a radical development, it has sometimes been criticised as amounting only to a bandaid approach to the problem of domestic violence, failing to tackle the root cause. On this view, as long as the emphasis is on providing emergency accommodation rather than attacking patriarchal assumptions, male violence will continue. Sawer and Simms take the argument one step further and suggest that, from some points of view, 'WEL women, by publicly lobbying for women's rights . . . may seem to be more radical than the liberationist doing her roster duty for the women's refuge collective' (1984: 189).

THE TWIN CONCERNS: HOUSING AND VIOLENCE

The preceding disagreements suggest that the attempt to categorise the refuge movement as reformist or revolutionary, or even to understand it in terms of a tension between these goals, may obscure more than it illuminates. In our view it is more useful to see the refuge movement as pursuing two purposes: to provide accommodation for women escaping violence, and to publicise and work towards the elimination of violence by men against women in the home. The two goals are quite distinct and at times almost incompatible. Much of the history and experience of the refuge movement is best understood in terms of the interplay between these purposes and the differing emphases which have been placed on them.

Take for a start the experience of the refuge workers themselves. Their changing preoccupations with respect to these concerns are vividly described in Johnson's account of the Marrickville women's refuge: 'Our original purpose in setting up refuges was to expose the dark underside of patriarchy's attitudes to women in marriage—the plight of the battered women' (1981: 1). But how was this to be done? There seemed little hope of persuading the police to intervene more effectively. Nor did there seem much likelihood of getting government funding to confront domestic violence head on. Their solution was to argue that victims of domestic violence were 'homeless in the sense that they were forced to remain in intolerable situtations because they had nowhere else to go' (1981: 2). Defining the problem as one of homelessness was more likely to attract government funds and, once refuges were established, their very existence would place the issue of wife bashing on the public agenda. In fact, however, as Johnson admits, homelessness was so far from being a key issue in the minds of the founders of the Marrickville refuge that an original list of ways in which they expected to be able to help women who came to the refuge did not include assistance with housing (1981: 7).

All this changed after the refuge opened its doors and was soon filled to overflowing. The need to re-house these women after their stay at the refuge became of paramount concern. Unless they could be moved on into permanent housing, the refuge would be unable to provide crisis accommodation for the continuing stream of women and children being referred to it. The energies of workers were thus diverted into efforts to persuade governments to provide re-housing. People given 'priority' by the New South Wales Housing Commission still had to wait three years for the allocation of a house, and refuge workers spent a great deal of time making written representations to the Commission to have the victims of violence treated as exceptional cases and given housing immediately. Despite hundreds of such representations, Johnson writes, 'only a handful of residents were given an out-of-turn allocation—and then only after waiting for months' (1981: 8). In an effort to deal with this problem the refuge also waged a long drawn out campaign for the allocation of a half-way house at Waterloo, which was finally conceded by the Housing Commision in 1977.

Since that time the New South Wales Housing Commission has taken several steps to meet the accommodation needs of women escaping violence. An emergency accommodation unit was set up in 1981 to lease out vacant government houses to community groups, to be run as refuges and half-way houses, and victims of violence are now automatically entitled to government housing on an out-of-turn basis (NSW Domestic Violence Committee, 1985: 66). Moreover, government tenants who are victims of violence 'have a right to be transferred immediately to alternative accommodation of their choice, or to have their existing tenancy transferred to their name, with their spouse being transferred elsewhere' (NSW Women's Advisory Council, 1987: 181).

Johnson admits that the refuge movement's intitial emphasis on wife bashing shifted to questions of housing and pensions, the most pressing matters facing refuge residents. But far from bewailing this as a retreat into reformism or a bandaid approach to the problem, she suggests that housing should properly be seen as a key issue for feminism:

> The women who come to the refuges ... are true revolutionary feminists, because they are women who have taken the most radical step possible in their own lives and in so doing have brought economic and social pressure to bear on the system to change in a direction which gives them and their children an alternative to dependence on men. Until these alternatives exist, all women, whether we know it or not, are essentially homeless and dispossessed. (1981: 16)

The interplay of the movement's dual purposes can also be traced in the annual reports of Beryl, the Canberra Women's Refuge. These reports provide some of the best documentation available on the processes at work within the refuge movement. Inspired by the Glebe refuge, a committee was formed in June 1974 and was given a house by the Department of the Capital Territory in March 1975. Along with ten other refuges, funding for a coordinator's salary was received in the middle of the year.

The primacy of the issue of homelessness is evident in the first report. In July 1975 the committee was offered, and accepted, a second building to use as a half-way house for women moving out of the refuge. Even so, accommodation pressures were such that in 1976 the government provided alternative premises for the refuge, twice the size of the original house. The report notes that large numbers of homeless adolescent girls were finding their way to the refuge and that there were conflicts between these girls and the mothers with children. It concludes that there is an urgent need for more women's refuges, adolescent refuges, half-way houses and more low-cost accommodation.

The second report, for 1977, takes up these themes. The presence in the refuge of single women, who are there for reasons not immediately to do with violence, is again raised but not resolved. There is also an account in the report of a submission made to government about the urgent housing needs of women and children in the ACT and a description of a squatting campaign on behalf of a woman who had been evicted from her government home because of inability to pay her rent. Refuge workers accompanied every woman who came to the refuge in need of emergency housing to the housing branch of the Department of the Capital Territory and helped her put her case for special consideration. Over time this steady pressure led to major improvements in the way the department dealt with such cases. Here was grassroots activism at its most effective!

But in addition to housing and funding issues, the refuge made a major submission to the Attorney-General concerning domestic violence. It recommended that the law should recognise the right of a woman and her children to live in the family home, and urged that violent men should be evicted. It also suggested that the police be more active in telling women about their rights in situations of violence. The submission was widely disseminated and had a substantial impact. Refuge workers were invited to talk about it to various groups and presented their views to the assistant police commissioner. One outcome of this meeting was that they were asked to lecture about the refuge to police cadets during their training. Thus, although the housing issue remained a pressing one, the refuge was beginning to devote some of its resources to the question of domestic violence itself.

Much of the accommodation pressure experienced by the refuge was due to the children; there were often twice as many children as women in residence. In 1978 the refuge was granted the house next door to use as a 'children's annex'. The new premises enabled the refuge to provide specialised day-care for babies and toddlers and to operate an after-school programme for older children, thus relieving some of the pressure in the refuge itself.

But the need for crisis accommodation for single women continued to plague Beryl and to divert resources from the issue of domestic violence. The refuge clearly wanted to shed this aspect of its work and in 1981 wrote a submission to government requesting funding for a separate single women's shelter. They were successful, and the new refuge opened in 1982. At last, Beryl was able to institute a policy of accepting only women who were escaping violence, thus sharpening its focus on the issue which had originally motivated its establishment.

Meanwhile, the stories told by the women who came to the refuge led to a growing realisation of the close connection between domestic violence and incest, involving both the sexual abuse by the violent man of his own children and the abuse of the women herself as a child. One direct outcome of this new awareness was a book, *Father–Daughter Rape,* written by one of the workers (Ward, 1985). In 1983 the refuge wrote a submission to government for funds to set up an incest counselling service. Again, it was successful, and the Incest Centre was established in 1984, initially with Beryl as its parent body. The new service counselled individual victims of incest and in addition had an educational role, its workers visiting schools and talking to students; it was not involved in the provision of accommodation.

Beryl's annual report for 1984–85 talks of an increasing role for refuge workers in organising and participating in domestic violence workshops in the wider community, as well as in making submissions to a variety of goverment organisations and inquiries, specifically about the problem of domestic violence.

In this brief account of Beryl's history we can see the interplay of the twin concerns of domestic violence and homelessness. While the former provided the motivation for the establishment of the refuge, the latter became the most pressing day-to-day issue, once in operation. But the refuge managed to avoid being entirely swamped by the accommodation needs of homeless women and to direct some of its resources into the growing movement against domestic violence. By the mid-1980s it had a high profile in the Canberra community, not just as a shelter for battered women, but also as a group lobbying for change in the way society and its legal institutions respond to male violence in the home.

The development of the refuge movement to encompass more than just the provision of emergency accommodation is also documented in some of the refuge evaluations which have been done by or for state governments. A 1986 Victorian report (Feldman, 1986) notes that individual refuges have devoted energy and resources to educating the public about domestic violence and incest. Workers have spoken to community groups and to schools, been involved in the writing and distribution of pamphlets about domestic violence and even contributed to the production of two films: *Women Breakout* and *No Myth*. In 1986, at the initiative of refuge workers, a Domestic Violence and Incest Resource Centre was opened in Melbourne, with the aim of publicising these two abuses (Feldman, 1986: 28).

THE FIGHT FOR FUNDING

One of the factors which certainly retarded the development of a focus on domestic violence was the threat to funding which the refuge movement had to fight, almost from the outset. At the end of 1975, just five months after its decision to fund refuges, the Whitlam Labor government was dismissed from office and replaced by a conservative coalition committed to a reduction in federal spending and to a philosophy of handing over a variety of financial responsibilities to the states. In 1976, the new government cut its funding for refuges to 90 per cent of operating costs and 75 per cent of capital costs. A year later these figures were cut to 75 per cent and 50 per cent respectively. The expectation was that the states would fund the difference. In New South Wales, Victoria and South Australia, state governments did just that, but in Western Australia and Queensland conservative governments initially refused, requiring the refuges to raise the money themselves. Eventually these two governments agreed to fund half the gap left by the federal withdrawal, but only if the refuges could somehow make up the difference (McFerren, 1987: 30–4).

The refuges could see that they were fighting for their lives. The action taken in 1977 alone gives some indication of the magnitude of their response. Canberra refuge workers devoted considerable time during the year to telephoning around Australia to assemble information on refuge needs and then to preparing a budget sub- mission outlining how they would like to see Commonwealth fund- ing for refuges operate. In May a refuge worker, along with representatives of other women's groups, met with the Prime Min- ister and spoke to him specifically about refuges. A nationally coordinated demonstration was held in June, including a sit-in at the Department of Health in Canberra, to draw attention to the plight the refuges would be in if funding ceased. In August, women from refuges around Australia demonstrated outside Parliament House on budget day and gained good media coverage.

These actions were surprisingly successful. Total federal funding grew considerably between 1975 and 1978, although because the number of refuges was increasing rapidly, it was spread more thinly. Dowse observes that, by contrast, the amount of money going to Aboriginal housing over the same period decreased by 81 per cent (1984: 151). 'Funding for women's refuges was in fact one of the few areas of Commonwealth expenditure ... to increase substantially during this time' (Dowse, 1984: 151).

The funding situation remained in doubt, however, because the federal government was still committed to handing over financial responsibility to the states. The 1980–81 budget saw further reduc- tions in direct Commonwealth grants and in 1981–82, after months of speculation and assurances to the contrary, all direct federal funding ceased. The states were now expected to finance women's refuges from their general health budgets and the fight for funding shifted to the state level. (See McFerren, 1987: 36–40, for an account of the Western Australian experience.)

The return of the Labor Party to power in the federal sphere in 1983 brought welcome relief to the refuge movement. Federal funds were again forthcoming with an immediate grant of $4 million and this, along with continued state support, meant that the financial situation of the refuges improved considerably. The federal funds were made available under a new Women's Emerg- ency Services Program (WESP) which, as its name implies, was not restricted to the provision of accommodation, but covered advice and support services such as rape crisis and incest centres. Here at last was government recognition that the issue of violence against women was not simply a matter of homelessness and that the solution to the problem involved more than just the provision of emergency accommodation. (These details are taken from a paper prepared by OSW on women's services, 1984.)

In January 1985 the government introduced a new Supported Accommodation Assistance Program (SAAP) designed to rationalise its various initiatives in this area. WESP was included as a sub-programme, along with sub-programmes for youth, Aborigines, single men and other special groups. This development met with vigorous resistance from women's groups, because the name of the new programme suggested that funding was once again to be restricted to the provision of crisis accommodation. The protests were unsuccessful in preventing the inclusion of WESP within SAAP, but successful in that it was conceded that WESP should continue to fund non-accommodation services. So the Women's Emergency Services Program retained its broader focus and the bureaucrats achieved their 'rationalisation' (Ford, 1988: 2). The anomolous provision of non-accommodation services under an accommodation programme was thus an outcome of bureaucratic compromise.

This broader focus of the women's programme enabled the rapid growth of non-accommodation services likely to bring the problem of domestic violence more clearly into focus. Between January 1985 and June 1987, the number of rape crisis and incest support services receiving federal funds increased from two to seven. In the same period the number of refuge referral and information services increased from four to nine. Throughout this period the women's programme was also funding four domestic violence crisis services aimed at migrant women (Ford, 1988). Unfortunately, from July 1989, SAAP ceased to fund new non-accommodation services, although it retained responsibility for services already in existence. New services would need to apply to the states for funding. Yet again, the central government was invoking the principles of federalism to limit its role.

INTEGRATION INTO THE COMMUNITY

Quite apart from the objectives being pursued by the refuge movement, the very existence of refuges and their increasing institutionalisation and integration into the community has had the effect of bringing the issue of domestic violence to the attention of an ever-widening audience. To demonstrate this point we turn again to the records of the Canberra Women's Refuge.

The first report speaks of a constant stream of visitors including members of parliament, journalists, and bureaucrats, all of whom would have taken away a message of the terrible reality of wife battering. In 1978 a group of Liberal Party women, including the wives of the two local federal members of parliament, came to paint one of the rooms. Such a visit would have had a profound impact on the women concerned.

The refuge has also developed important links with the service clubs such as Lions, Rotary, and Quota. Workers regularly speak at club functions and have often received financial assistance from them. Links have been forged with a host of other community groups, government departments and legal agencies in the process of dealing with residents' problems. The report for 1981–82 lists, in addition to schools, police, legal aid and the family court, no less than 22 government agencies and 19 voluntary organisations with whom the refuge interacted during the year.

Refuge workers are also unionised and in 1982 the Canberra refuge established a closed shop, that is, made union membership a condition of employment. In this way the refuge movement has attracted union protection and been able to negotiate for award wages. However, the award under which they are covered is not specifically for refuge workers and, with the assistance of the Australian Social Welfare Union, the movement has continued to press for an award specifically tailored to refuge work. The fact that refuge workers around Australia went on strike in 1982 over the funding issue (Scutt, 1983: 270) is a further illustration of their increasing integration into the labour movement.

Such evidence suggests that refuges had become thoroughly embedded in the community and thoroughly enmeshed in the welfare and industrial relations systems. These myriad points of contact between the refuges and the society ensured that the issue of violence against women would move increasingly onto the public agenda.

There is yet another way in which the presence of refuges in the society contributed to the progress of the movement against domestic violence. At the beginning in the 1980s, state governments began to launch inquiries into domestic violence with the aim of reforming the law in this area. As already indicated, refuge activities had highlighted the many deficiencies in the way the legal system dealt with violence against women, and numerous submissions had been made to governments. But more than this, once the inquiries got under way, refuge workers had an obvious part to play. In some cases they were invited to sit as full members of the inquiry; for example, two of the members of the 1981 New South Wales Task Force were refuge workers, as was one member of the 1988 Queensland Task Force. In other cases, where the inquiry had to be conducted by lawyers, refuge workers served as consultants, as happened with the ACT Law Reform Commission inquiry which reported in 1986. It is hard to imagine more eloquent testimony to the role of the refuge movement in focusing public attention on domestic violence.

REFUGE ORGANISATION

The issue of refuge organisation remains to be addressed. It is relevant to the concerns of this chapter in two ways. First, it is in its organisational forms, rather than in the goals it pursues, that the refuge movement can lay the most meaningful claim to radicalism. Second, it is sometimes argued that the nature of refuge organisation impedes the movement's effectiveness in bringing about social change. We do not wish to endorse this argument but merely to examine it.

The underlying assumption of radical feminism, indeed the radical wing of many movements for social change, is that the hierarchical institutions of society oppress and disempower people, making them unable to take control of their own lives. On this view, real social change depends on countering these forces and working to empower the individual. Thus it is not enough to remove a woman from violence, or even to change the laws relating to violence, important though these may be. The ultimate aim must be to help women make their own choices, even if the choice is to remain with a violent man. To this end refuge workers must provide support but not expert advice or direction. They must function as women who share a common form of oppression, not as professionals with superior knowledge. (The second annual report of the Canberra refuge contains an impressive statement of this philosophy.)

The collective form of organisation is the logical outcome of such thinking; it is the standard form of organisation in feminist refuges. The collective consists of the paid and volunteer workers and sometimes outsiders with an interest in the refuge. It does not usually include the residents. Within the collective there is no organisational hierarchy and decisions are made by consensus. Records are open, information is shared and there are no designated spokeswomen. Jobs are rotated and day-to-day decisions are made as far as possible by those affected and not by groups or individuals separated from the daily round of activities.

For refuge workers in particular, the processes by which the group operates are regarded as more important than the particular tasks at hand. If violence has its roots in hierarchy, as the theory of patriarchy suggests, then non-hierarchical, empowering forms of organisation are an integral part of the struggle against domestic violence.

For many women, working in collectives has indeed been an empowering and radicalising experience. Here are the words of one such worker:

> The experience of working in a feminist collective is an exciting and empowering one, learning new skills and sharing responsibilities, talking and questioning with other women. It is part of my aim of personal liberation, which is part of the struggle for the liberation of all women. (Younger, 1986: 260)

But there is also a down side. Organisations which lack a formal hierarchy invariably develop informal ones. These may be benign, but can also be just as oppressive as any formal structure. The whole phenomenon has been well analysed by Freeman, in her article, 'The Tyranny of Structurelessness' (1973). Moreover, the absence of people designated to speak on behalf of the group has led to a sense of frustration on the part of bureaucrats seeking to establish contact or negotiate with refuges. They complain that they often feel unsure of whom they are talking to and unable to assume any continuity in communication.

More importantly from the point of view of governments which fund the refuges, the collective form of organisation can lead to a lack of accountability. Several refuges and rape crisis services have been at least temporarily defunded because of what was viewed by government as financial irresponsibility. The matter has been nicely analysed by Ford (1988) in a review of the Women's Emergency Services Program conducted for the federal government. She argues that 'some of the major conflicts in WESP have arisen over the operation, or as a result, of collectives'. She then makes a distinction between 'management' and day-to-day operations and argues that the problem lies with the former:

> Broadly, management functions involve establishing service objectives, employment of staff, program accountability and operation. It is certainly possible to undertake these tasks collectively, but problems appear to arise when the collective is solely a worker collective. The development of worker-only collectives is a result of the increasing number of paid staff in refuges. In the early years of the program, all refuges relied on the support and active participation of a number of people who were not paid. In feminist services, many of these people had close links with the broader women's movement; this not only brought a constant influx of new ideas but also provided a diverse group to oversee the operation of the service and provide accountability to government and the wider women's movement. With the increasing numbers of paid staff and the more autonomous nature of the women's refuge program, some worker-only collectives developed. These run the grave risks of becoming very inward looking and being torn apart by the tensions of playing both employer and employee roles. (1988: 16)

Ford goes on to advocate that such collectives be broadened by the inclusion of other women not on the payroll. This would enable them to carry out their management functions to the satisfaction of government.

Another aspect of the collective philosophy which has affected relationships with government is the question of national organisation. Of course, the movement would not countenance a national hierarchy with office holders and spokeswomen. Nevertheless, national coordination was obviously necessary. A loose association of refuges, the National Confederation of Women's Refuges, was formed in 1976 and the first National Conference of Women's Refuges was held in Melbourne in 1978 (see Beryl annual reports).

But the absence of any national organisation at the outset proved to be an irritant for the federal government. Just prior to the Whitlam government's 1975 decision to fund the eleven refuges then in existence or about to open, Women's Affairs officials tried to get the refuges to join a loose national confederation to facilitate the delivery of funds. Such an organisation would have enabled funds to go direct to the refuges; in its absence the funds would have to be channelled through state bureaucracies, some of which were hostile to the refuges and might therefore cause problems (Dowse, 1984: 153). At least one refuge, the Half-way House in Melbourne, declined to join and wrote to the Prime Minister objecting to the way the government was trying to force refuges into a confederation which 'would probably include organisations with conflicting aims and policies' (quoted in Dowse, 1984: 154). The plan was defeated and Dowse, a former head of the Office of Women's Affairs, regards the attitudes expressed by the Half-way House collective as having jeopardised their funding. She laments the 'refuges' suspicion of the bureaucracy and the inability of many of them to look beyond the immediate needs of their individual collectives', and she describes the Half-way House as behaving 'like a libertarian classroom in an authoritarian school' (1984: 153–4). 'Too often [she writes] feminist collectives operating women's services have measured their political efficacy by . . . how well they function as collectives . . . and this has produced a degree of shortsightedness' (1984: 147–8).

It is clear, then, that the collective form of organisation has at times strained the relationship between refuges and the governments that fund them. This has sometimes proved fatal for particular refuges. But whether this tension has ultimately been to the detriment of the refuge movement as a whole is hard to say. The final position taken in the goverment's 1988 review of refuges is that collectives, properly constituted, are effective forms of management and should be encouraged.

It remains to be said that the preceding discussion in no way constitutes an overall evaluation of collectives; it is concerned only with their relationships with government and the relevance this may have for the progress of the refuge movement. Any complete evaluation would need to take account of the possibilities of personal empowerment and the potential for the radical transformation of society, which are the ultimate justification of this form of organisation.

CONCLUSION

This chapter has traced the development of the refuge movement and shown how it has increasingly drawn public attention to the issue of domestic violence. This has not, however, been an uninterrupted process. The movement has at times seemed to be little more than a crisis accommodation service, and in the latter part of the 1970s it became, inevitably, preoccupied with the fight for funding. Indeed, it is clear that the progress of the movement has been related to, although not entirely dependent on, the fortunes of the federal Labor Party. Both the initial funding and the expansion into non-accommodation services were facilitated by the presence of Labor governments in Canberra. This is a theme to which we shall return in later chapters. But through it all, the refuge movement managed to devote some of its resources to publicising and combating domestic violence and it has clearly been a major contributor to the emergence of domestic violence in the 1980s as an issue of public concern. Another important factor in this process has been the activity of feminists in the bureaucracy, and it is to this subject that we now turn.

3   The femocrats

The previous chapter looked at the role of the refuge movement in drawing attention to domestic violence; this chapter will examine the contribution of feminists in government bureaucracy—femocrats, as they have come to be called. To begin with, we must again go back to the early days of the contemporary women's movement.

At the outset, second-wave feminism in Australia was a grassroots movement, an assemblage of small groups, organised locally and with a focus on local activities. In so far as it turned to the state, it did so from the outside, and with the purpose of making demands upon the state—demands for funding, for new policies and for new legislation. Even the Women's Electoral Lobby, formed in 1972 with the express purpose of influencing the state, sought to do so essentially from the outside.

All this began to change in 1973 when the Prime Minister appointed Elizabeth Reid as his first women's advisor. When the new position was advertised in December 1972, it divided the movement. Reid and the 450-odd women who applied for the job 'felt it was a challenge needing a response. For the first time in our history [she writes], we were being offered the opportunity to attempt to implement what for years we had been writing, yelling, marching and working towards. Not to respond would have felt as if our bluff had been called' (1987: 12). The other view was that the creation of this and other women's positions in the bureaucracy would begin a process of co-option which would ultimately disempower the movement.

The year following Reid's appointment, a Women's Affairs Section was established within the Department of Prime Minister and Cabinet, to support the women's advisor (Dowse, 1983: 205), and since that time a network of government bodies has been established at state and federal level to promote the interests of women. In just a few years a flourishing femocracy had become an established part of the apparatus of government. Women were now in a position to assert their interests from within the bureaucracy as well as outside it. (For more extensive histories see Ryan, 1990, and Sawer, 1990.)

The extent to which feminism has made inroads into government—and we are talking here not just about individual feminists but about bodies set up to represent women's interests and staffed largely by self-identified feminists—has been far greater in Australia than in other countries. It is no coincidence that the term 'femocrat' is an Australian creation.

Why this should be so is an intriguing question which we shall not pursue in detail here. It is worth noting, however, that the emergence of a femocracy is symptomatic of a more general Australian tendency to integrate social movements into the fabric of the state. The classic example of this is the way the Australian labour movement has pursued its goals by becoming a part of the state apparatus to a degree almost unequalled elsewhere in the world. The centralised wage-fixing system, the existence of Labor governments, and the practice of tripartitism—the control of state organisations such as the Occupational Health and Safety Commission by three parties: government, business and the unions—all illustrate the point.

THE FEMOCRAT DEBATE

The debate over the femocrat strategy as a means of pursuing women's interests is in part the well-known ideological debate between liberal/reformist and radical feminism. The radical view is that the state is essentially a patriarchal state, that is, *in principle,* it can do no other than represent male interests. It is therefore counter-productive or, at best, pointless to work within the bureaucracy, as the femocrats have chosen to do. Anne Game puts it thus:

> Feminists face a dilemma in developing strategies for state intervention: how can demands be made on the state to intervene in the interests of women when the state embodies the interests of men? If the state is not neutral and benevolent with respect to women, is a challenge to patriarchy possible through state activity? (Game, 1985: 167, cited in Franzway et al., 1989: 27).

The argument takes various forms. One is that the oppression of women by men is related to hierarchical forms of organisation. It is this analysis which has led women to adopt the collective as their preferred mode of organisation. On this view, to work within a bureaucratic hierarchy, as the femocrats are obliged to do, cannot contribute to the personal empowerment of women and so can do nothing to undermine patriarchal domination. Here are the words of one former femocrat who endorses this view:

> The most serious contradiction I observed was between ideology and

structural position, between senior women working for equal rights legislation and their subordinates. Senior women often treated women lower in their bureaucratic hierarchy contrary to what I would regard as socialist-feminist principles of respecting and supporting other women, negating hierarchies, allowing women the power to define themselves and their work and working collectively with self-conscious but open political purpose. (Johnson, quoted in Franzway, 1986: 53).

A second form of this 'in principle' argument is that the very objectivity and impersonality of the procedures by which the state operates are, in principle, patriarchal. For instance, it has been suggested that the legal process is patriarchal in its very objectivity. 'When it most closely conforms to precedent, to facts, to legislative intent, it will most closely enforce socially male norms ... Abstract rights will authorize the male experience of the world' (MacKinnon, 1983: 658, cited in Franzway et al., 1989: 29).

This is not the place to develop these arguments in detail, nor, indeed, to critique them. But it must be noted that they are somewhat problematic. Hierarchy is not always disempowering. Universities, which are certainly hierarchical organisations, frequently offer courses—women's studies, for example—which prove to be empowering and radicalising for the students who enrol. Again, as Franzway et al. point out (1989: 30), legal tribunals such as those concerned with equal employment opportunity and anti-discrimination legislation have repeatedly found in favour of women in the face of stiff opposition from patriarchal interests.

It is these kinds of objections which inform the liberal/reformist position of the femocrats. The femocrat strategy assumes that the state, while frequently reinforcing the interests of men, is not inherently gendered, that is, is not inherently a patriarchal institution. It is therefore worthwhile infiltrating the state apparatus and using it to further women's interests. Men will resist this process and the fact that many of the top position holders in government are men will make the battle a difficult one. Moreover, there are still numerous, subtle ways in which apparently gender-neutral bureaucratic procedures discriminate against women; for example, the preference for filling positions on a full-time rather than part-time basis which, given the present division of domestic labour, tends to favour male workers. But the situation is not, in principle, hopeless. Femocrats make the point over and over again that without the active support of a strong women's movement outside the bureaucracy, women on the inside face an almost impossible task; but with that support, significant progress is possible.

Quite apart from the argument that the state is inherently, or in principle patriarchal, there are other criticisms which are sometimes made of the femocrat strategy and femocrats. One of these is that the experience of working in the bureaucracy is likely to undermine the commitment of femocrats to feminism and that over time they come to see themselves as serving different interests. Here are the words of one femocrat who acknowledges this process:

> I am a bureaucrat. The community regards me as a bureaucrat and so I'm distrusted, and rightly so. I'd feel the same way. I have loyalties, obligations and duties to the department. I take them lightly but I can't take them too lightly. I also have an obligation to the taxpayer and the community that I work effectively and responsibly. We're caught in the middle. (Singh, quoted in Franzway et al., 1989: 141)

One of the best known critics of the femocrat strategy makes the point rather more polemically:

> There is nothing more insidious than the paranoia and caution that sets in on anyone who has been there more than a year or so. This can only be halted by the infusion of new people, and perhaps some willing to accept short-term appointments, who will not thereby be overwhelmed by the general elitism, chauvinism, authoritarianism and secretiveness of the Public Service. (Pringle, quoted in Franzway et al., 1989: 141)

A further criticism of femocrats often made by the wider women's movement relates to their class location. They occupy high-status, highly-paid positions with attractive career opportunities. This puts them in a very different class position from the majority of women. One outcome of this is that, although they may claim to be working on behalf of all women, in practice the benefits they seek may only be relevant to a restricted class of women. For example, as Game points out, affirmative action programmes which have been such a focus of femocrat activity, while clearly enhancing the career prospects of women in a variety of bureaucratic and professional jobs, do nothing for the outworkers in the garment industry or women on the assembly lines (1984, cited in Franzway, 1986: 50). Summers claims that femocrats are sometimes even 'accused of making money out of the plight of women less economically privileged than themselves' (1986: 60). On this view, then, femocrats tend to represent the interests, not of all women, but of a particular class of women.

Again, this is not the place to evaluate these views in detail. Nor do we necessarily endorse them. We have outlined them simply to give some indication of the controversy which has surrounded the development of the femocrat strategy.

FEMOCRATS BELEAGUERED

The preceding criticisms have certainly stung the women who

occupy bureaucratic positions, and the result is that they often end up feeling isolated from the women's movement and misunderstood and unappreciated. The resentment is palpable in the following passage written by Anne Summers who, as head of the Office of the Status of Women, was for a time Australia's top femocrat:

> Instead of these appointments (women's advisers) being greeted by the women's movement with approval, they have tended to cause confusion or consternation. Interestingly, the criticism has been directed more at the appointees than at the governments that have responded in this manner to women's political pressure ... There has been an almost unwholesome eagerness to find fault with such appointees, to criticise them for what they say, for their silences, even for their clothes ... It is noteworthy that similar criticisms are seldom directed at the relatively large numbers of women who have been elected to state and federal parliaments over the past decade ... Nor is the same criticism made of women who are appointed to high-ranking public service positions in other areas of the bureaucracy. By contrast, such appointments are usually welcomed and seen as evidence of progress.

Summers captures the sense of isolation in her description of how femocrats are seen: either as 'Missionaries' or as 'Mandarins':

> ... most other sections of the bureaucracy regard women's advisers as Missionaries, as an unprofessional political intrusion into a career system that regards itself as having no political allegiances beyond perhaps the corporate view of the department concerned. Women's advisers are seen as barrow-pushers and ideologues who are incapable of delivering impartial advice. At the same time, many in the women's movement regard women's advisers as Mandarins (career bureaucrats), more intent on playing bureaucratic games than in serving their sisters. (1986: 62)

Summers concludes that 'women's advisers need to be both Mandarins and Missionaries', and she laments the fact that 'the tension between the two roles will for the forseeable future remain an occupational hazard for femocrats' (1986: 67).

The femocrats' feeling of isolation from the women's movement, even rejection by it, is evident in the rather strange title of an article written by another former head of the then federal Office of Women's Affairs, Sara Dowse: 'The Bureaucrat as Usurer'. Dowse describes the role of the usurer, or money lender, in pre-capitalist Europe: it was vital for the economic life of the society, but despised as being contrary to the teachings of Christianity. Such employment was consequently restricted to a class of untouchables—the Jews. Bureaucrats, and in particular femocrats, she suggests, play a similarly vital but despised role in modern society: vital, because all oppressed or disadvantaged groups must look to the state for the fulfilment of their hopes and aspirations, and despised, by sections of the women's movement, because of the compromises which bureaucrats inevitably make. Dowse's analogy, which at first seems unintelligible, acquires a wealth of meaning once we understand the anguish which generated it.

The tension between femocrats and the wider women's movement is clearly documented in relation to a funding issue which was raised in 1975, International Women's Year (IWY). The government had allocated a one-off grant of $2 million for IWY, and the Treasury was asking that all the new women's services— refuges, health centres etc.— which were applying for grants for the first time, be funded from this source. The women of the IWY Secretariat were fighting this and seeking to have the new women's projects taken on by various departments and funded out of departmental budgets. This would have ensured proper, ongoing funding for the new services and released the IWY money for other, one-off purposes (Dowse, 1984: 155).

But many women outside the bureaucracy felt betrayed by this manoeuvre, believing that the money should have been spent in accordance with the priorities already established by the women's movement and not on projects dreamed up by femocrats. Pringle and Game, advocates of this latter position, are ruthless in their criticism of Elizabeth Reid for her role in the affair: 'Reid was able to *manipulate* large sections of [the movement] into *sycophantic* support' of the IWY Secretariat (1976: 77, emphasis added). That such comments could be made in print gives some indication of the depth of feelings which existed on the issue and provides a real insight into the femocrats' view that they are isolated and misunderstood.

THE FEMOCRAT ROLE

Although femocrats are a part of the women's movement, their agenda is not a simple reflection of some broader women's movement agenda. Their location within government bureaucracy provides opportunities for action not open to women outside and poses questions not faced by other feminists. As Franzway puts it, they 'have problems of their own' (1986: 46). Femocrats are not simply the agents of the women's movement inside the bureaucracy, but it is not reasonable to conclude that their efforts are irrelevant to women's interests or even detrimental to them, as some commentators argue (Game and Pringle, 1976). A theme we shall be stressing in succeeding sections of this chapter is that, despite the tensions which we have described above, many of the achievements of the women's movement have depended on cooperation and constructive interaction between women inside and outside bureaucracy.

It is important to recognise that the femocrat role varies considerably, depending on the issue. We shall develop this point at some length so that the role femocrats have played in relation to domestic violence can be seen in a broader context. Take for example questions about the internal operations of government bureaucracy, whose importance for all women is largely unrecognised by the wider movement. On these issues femocrats must take the initiative and carry on the fight alone. By contrast, issues such as the funding of women's services are initiated and propelled by the wider women's movement and in relation to these questions femocrats are, in a sense, the agents of the movement inside the bureaucracy. In describing femocrats as agents in such matters we are not intending to belittle their importance. Agents are often vital to the successful articulation of the interests of individuals and groups on whose behalf they work. We use the term simply to convey the fact that in such matters it is women's groups outside the bureaucracy, not the femocrats, who are the real driving force. Of course, most issues fall somewhere between the two extremes, involving initiatives from both inside and outside the bureaucracy.

Domestic violence is not an issue intrinsic to the bureaucracy; it is a concern of the wider women's movement. We hope to show, later, that it was only taken up by femocrats as community pressures began to be felt. Before doing so, however, we propose to discuss various examples of femocrat activity in terms of this role variability we have identified.

FEMOCRATS AS INITIATORS

An example of femocrats acting as initiators is the question of how femocracy itself should be organised within the federal public service. A great deal of femocrat energy went into this issue, particularly in the mid-1970s. Elizabeth Reid's support staff was located in the Department of Prime Minister and Cabinet (PM&C), but it was widely recognised that women's issues occurred throughout government and that there was a fight to be fought in every government department. The femocrat strategy was therefore to set up a network of women's units in key departments, coordinated by the Women's Affairs Section of PM&C (Dowse, 1983: 212). The strategy was largely successful and by December 1977 there were eleven women's units in various departments, in addition to the now renamed Office of Women's Affairs (OWA) in PM&C. (Dowse, 1981: 11). But just as the strategy appeared about to bear fruit, it was undermined by bureaucrats hostile to the women's movement who persuaded the government to downgrade

and transfer the OWA to a newly created and peripheral Department of Home Affairs, where it could no longer carry out the vital
task of monitoring Cabinet submissions for their effects on women
(Dowse, 1983: 213). Its head, Sara Dowse, resigned in protest.
This organisational defeat continued to hamper the femocracy
until OWA's return to the Prime Minister's department, this time as
the Office of the Status of Women (OSW), following Labor's re-
election in 1983.

A second femocrat concern, of far-reaching significance for
women but of little interest outside government circles, is the
budget programme which the OSW was able to implement in 1984
(Summers, 1986: 65). The programme coordinates information
from every department on the impact on women of all government
activity. It is presented in the form of a budget paper. The women's
budget programme has resulted in the provision of a great deal of
new information and, in addition, has sensitised individual departments to the effect of their activities on women. The head of OSW
provides an example of this process of sensitisation (Brooks,
1986). She notes that initially when the Trade, Industry, Tech-
nology and Commerce portfolios were approached by OSW, the
response was that their policies were 'gender neutral'. In subsequent years they began to look more seriously at the issue and
acknowledged, for example, that the industries most likely to be
affected by the proposed reduction in tariff barriers were also
major employers of women. In the textile, clothing and footwear
industry, for instance, one of the industries most threatened by
tariff reductions, 70 per cent of the total workforce is female. As a
result of this information, made available under the budget
programme, OSW has actively promoted assistance for workers
retrenched in this industry.

Femocrats are in complete agreement as to the importance of the
budget programme. Sawer (1989: 47) believes it to be one of the
distinctive achievements of Australian feminists, which has
enabled the women's movement to make greater progress in Australia than elsewhere. Dowse (1989: 8) agrees, and Summers
regards its inauguration as one of the most important achievements of her period as head of the OSW (see also Sharp and
Broomhill, 1990). But despite the importance of the women's
budget programme, a book-length treatment of femocrats written
by three academics and published in 1989 failed to mention it
(Franzway et al.). It is ironic that, outside the bureaucracy, this is
one of the least visible of femocrat initiatives.

Equal Employment Opportunity (EEO) is yet another example,
we would argue, of femocrats acting as initiators. There is a certain
irony here. EEO was amongst the first demands made by the

women's movement as a whole. One of the earliest women's liberation demonstrations was against sexist job advertising, and WEL began lobbying for anti-discrimination legislation in 1974 (Franzway et al., 1989: 89). But women in government took up this cause with a vengeance—after all it was their own cause—and anti-discrimination legislation was enacted in several states in the 1970s. Federally, annual reports reveal that the Office of Women's Affairs was active throughout the years of the Fraser government, from 1975 to 1983, lobbying for anti-discrimination legislation and, in particular, for equal employment opportunity. Indeed, in 1980 the federal government launched its EEO guidelines, aimed at all employers. Federal anti-discrimination legislation was passed in 1984, following the return of Labor to power. Moreover, first at the state level and later at the federal, units were established aimed at promoting EEO within government itself, and a great deal of femocrat energy has been expended on this project.

In reaction to all of this, numbers of feminists outside government now view EEO, and particularly EEO officers in government, with suspicion. The policy itself is criticised as being merely reformist: it does nothing to tackle hierarchy and elitism and does not really get at the fundamental processes of patriarchal oppression. As for EEO officers themselves, 'charges of elitism, co-option, management style, poor management, self-interest, antiunionism, and even criticisms of their dress (the silk shirt syndrome) have all been levelled' (Franzway et al., 1989: 102). Again, we do not wish to endorse these criticisms, but rather to use them as evidence of the degree to which EEO has become a femocrat initiative rather than a grassroots demand. We are not, of course, saying that EEO is no longer a concern of the broader movement, but simply that it is now the femocrats who are making the running (see, generally, Ronalds, 1990).

FEMOCRATS AS AGENTS

The story of the early days of childcare funding reveals feminist bureaucrats acting as agents of the broader movement rather than as independent initiators. (The following discussion draws on Dowse, 1983: 207–10). Childcare was seen by many sections of the movement as a key to the liberation of women from domestic slavery. As Dowse (1983: 218) puts it, 'the question of children remains the central issue for women ... [The provision of childcare] is a necessary condition of women's liberation, and the pursuit of it exposes the contradictions of patriarchal capitalism as no other campaign can.' Accordingly, the Whitlam Labor government was subjected to sustained lobbying during its first two years of office and, as a result, pledged in the 1974 election campaign to spend $130 million on a childcare programme. On re-election the government proposed to cut this back to $34 million, but after protests from WEL it compromised on $75 million. However, the money was earmarked not only for childcare but also for pre-schools, which do not see their function as freeing mothers to enter the workforce. These two interests, therefore, had to do battle for the funds. The pre-school lobby seemed set to take the lion's share of the funds when Elizabeth Reid intervened and was able to convince the Cabinet to seek further input and eventually to reverse its priorities. In this case, then, the femocrats' role was as the agent of the wider movement. We reiterate that this is not to belittle their contribution, for without the intervention of feminist bureaucrats, the demands of the movement stood little chance of being translated into policy.

REFUGE FUNDING

The role of federal femocrats in relation to refuge funding is a similar case. Women's groups were requesting funding throughout 1974 and 1975 and the Labor government was sympathetic. Officials in the Office of Women's Affairs (OWA) pushed to have the responsibility for the funding of refuges located in favourable departments and programmes, and the method of funding settled on in 1975 was via the Community Health Program (CHP). The disadvantage of this procedure was that CHP funds were distributed in the first instance to the states, to be passed on to the refuges. This exposed the refuges to the delaying tactics of hostile state governments. Things came to a head in 1977 when the Queensland government refused to pass on federal funds to the Brisbane and Townsville refuges, because of their alleged left-wing leanings. Femocrats and refuge workers alike protested vehemently, and the result was a government decision to fund the two refuges directly (Dowse, 1981: 13). OWA officials now sought to have the funding responsibility transferred to the Department of Social Security, where there were no constitutional impediments to funding the refuges directly. But the Department was unwilling and a crisis ensued in which it seemed, for a while, that the refuges would receive no funding at all.

OWA made representations to the Prime Minister, alerted the refuges and organised a media campaign. The refuges, as we saw in the last chapter, mounted an extensive campaign of their own. The result of these combined efforts was that funding was not only continued, but doubled. Responsibility for funding remained, however, with the CHP. On this point, the femocrats were defeated.

But the OWA could not ensure federal funding for much longer. As was mentioned in the last chapter, the Fraser government's philosophy of handing over financial responsibility to the states meant that by 1981 the states had full control over refuge funding. This did not, of course, mean the end of funding for the refuges. Many state governments were sympathetic to the refuge movement, and those that weren't found themselves forced by public opinion to maintain and even increase funding (McFerren, 1987: 39). Moreover, femocrats at the state level played a part in ensuring the continuation of funding, but that is beyond the scope of this discussion. It is worth recording Dowse's opinion, though, that 'the fortunes of women's services are tied, no matter how imperfectly, to the growth of these officials [at the state level], and to their increasing knowledge and expertise' (1984: 156).

Refuge funding, then, was an issue initiated and propelled by grassroots workers and facilitated by femocrats at the level of government. Let us reflect a little further on the femocrat contribution. At the outset it has to be acknowledged that the political leanings of the government of the day were an important factor. The presence of Labor in power from the end of 1972 to the end of 1975 clearly influenced the way the refuge issue emerged and was dealt with. Labor was sympathetic to funding requests from community groups and, furthermore, Labor had installed a fledgling femocracy which was then in a position to shepherd refuge funding requests through the bureaucracy. It is hard to imagine refuge funding getting under way with a conservative government in power, although it is quite possible that the refuge movement itself might have generated enough public pressure to force the conservatives to move in this direction. Certainly, once the conservatives came to government in 1975 the combined input of the refuge movement and its femocrat backers was enough to ensure the continuation of federal funding until the end of the 1970s. But neither of these groups could prevail in the longer term against Fraser's ideological commitment to decentralised funding. Finally, it was the return of Labor to power in 1983 which undoubtedly gave the refuge movement a new lease of life, at least financially. Anne Summers' own evaluation of the power of her office is consistent with this view: 'its varied ability to influence policy largely depend[ed] upon which party was in power' (1986: 61).

The greater sympathy of the ALP for women's concerns and its tendency to take more seriously the advice coming from women's units within the bureaucracy is not something we wish to examine in detail here. It needs to be said though that it is not simply that the ALP has been more aware than the conservatives of the electoral significance of women's issues. It is also the case that women's groups within the party have had considerable success in reforming party organisation (Sawer and Simms, 1984: 140). Affirmative action policies have resulted in a striking increase in the number of women at all levels of the party and the number of women selected to contest elections rose rapidly from 1977 onwards (Sawer and Simms, 1984: 109). At the time of writing three of the eight parliamentary leaders of the ALP at the state and territory level are women and all three have served as premier or chief minister. The point is, then, that the women's movement within the ALP must be counted as one of the factors which has enabled femocrats to wield greater influence under Labor governments than under the conservatives.

But given this political framework, what was the specific contribution of the femocrats? In our view, theirs was not the 'missionary' role described by Summers. Missionaries act in isolation from their backers and their success depends entirely on their own efforts. In the case of refuge funding it was the outside movement which persuaded the government to support the cause. The femocrats did not themselves apply the pressure; they channelled it to the points within the bureaucracy where it could have maximum effect and argued for the refuge requests in the terms most likely to be persuasive to senior bureaucrats and government ministers.

Dowse, who as head of the OWA was intimately involved in this process, writes as follows: 'The refuge funding crisis of 1977 became something of a success through the effective use of a double strategy involving the mobilisation of the women's bureaucratic apparatus and the refuges' network towards arousing public sympathy and applying political pressure' (1984: 158).

It is clear from this discussion that it was the cooperation between these two groups which enabled the movement to achieve the degree of success that it did. The activities of women inside and outside the bureaucracy were complementary. In distinguishing between the roles of grassroots workers and femocrats in the way we have we are not seeking to aportion credit for these achievements, but rather to illuminate the process by which, together, the two groups contributed to the momentum for change.

FEMOCRATS AND LAW REFORM

The role which femocrats play in relation to law reform often requires them to work as both agents and initiators. This is so for two reasons. First, while the impetus for law reform may come from grassroots demands, these cannot be translated directly into law but must be shaped to take account of legal considerations— constitutional matters, likely judicial interpretations, and so on. Femocrats involved in this process, especially the legally trained, are thus in a position to play a more creative and independent role than is involved, for instance, in simply putting the case for additional refuge funding. Secondly, new laws must be passed by parliament and are thus open to far more scrutiny by hostile sections of the community than is the case with mere administrative changes. For this reason, femocrats involved in the process must take into account the concerns of the politicians who will enact the law. The possibilities for departure from initial women's movement demands in this process are obvious. Indeed the process can lead women outside the bureaucracy to feel deeply betrayed by those within.

These points are well illustrated in Scutt's description (1985) of the process leading to the reform of the law of rape in New South Wales in 1980. She shows how grassroots demands led to a government commitment to reform, how women's groups were active in making submissions as to how the new law should be framed and how, in the final drafting stage, femocrats from the New South Wales government Women's Coordination Unit took over and gave the law their own stamp. Here is her description of that final stage (1985: 18):

> Bureaucrats effectively shut out community women's participation, second guessing what the politicians would want the law to be—and effectively cutting down the radical nature of the reform in a belief that the politicians would not 'wear it'. And especially regrettable, it was women bureaucrats who worked on the patriarchal side and were responsible for 'watering down' the feminists' demands.

Scutt reflects further on what happened (1985: 21):

> Was the [femocrat] failure to be supportive, and worse, their active subversion of feminist demands, the result of genuine inability to sum up the position correctly, so that for the sake of what reforms were possible (in their view) they tailored the demands to suit? Or were the bureaucratic games that were played the result of intoxication with the power they thought they wielded in advisory and governmental positions? Was there a desire to see the reform of the rape law as theirs alone, rather than the result of a massive movement, of cooperation between thousands of women?

Scutt tends towards the latter view. But whichever the case, her point is that femocrats betrayed the women's movement in the matter of rape law reform. Our point is a more limited one. It is that Scutt's account provides evidence of the way in which femocrats can depart from women's movement initiatives and follow agendas of their own in matters of law reform. It is for this reason that we see femocrat activity in relation to law reform as combining both the agent and initiator roles.

THE FEDERAL FEMOCRACY AND DOMESTIC VIOLENCE

One of the primary demands of the movement against domestic violence has been for law reform to enable the police and courts to intervene more effectively on behalf of victims. This demand has come in part from refuge workers and has been addressed to state governments, who are responsible for such legislation. Femocrats at the state level were thus involved in this process throughout the 1980s, but detailed accounts of their experience have yet to be written.

Some discussion of the situation at the state level has, however, been provided by McFerren (1990), who focuses on the experience in Western Australia and New South Wales. She notes that the political complexion of the government has significantly influenced the progress of the movement against domestic violence at the state level, facilitating it in New South Wales and hampering it in Western Australia. She also stresses, as we have, that despite the misunderstandings which have occurred at times between refuge workers (the frontline, as she calls them) and femocrats, one of the features of the movement has been the cooperation between these groups. She recounts how refuge workers 'took examples of police inaction and magisterial indifference to the Women's Co-ordination Unit, who advised the Premier to set up a task force into domestic violence' (1990: 202). The result was a report, issued in 1981, followed by legislative change. She concludes that 'any researched look at a history of the refuge programme, at least in New South Wales, shows the value of the relationship between the frontline and the feminist bureaucracy' (McFerren, 1990: 204).

At the federal level it was only in the late 1980s that the OSW became involved in the question of domestic violence specifically, as distinct from the issue of refuge funding. The question of refuge funding had been ongoing since the mid-1970s, and one of OSW's achievements in this area was to organise national conferences of refuge workers in 1978, 1981 and 1982, aimed at helping the refuges to speak with a single national voice (Sawer, 1990: 50). However, the annual reports of the office make scarcely a reference to the matter of domestic violence itself until the report for 1987–88 which announces a national campaign against domestic violence. We shall show in what follows that the appearance of domestic violence on the federal agenda was very much a result of input from the wider women's movement. (The following discussion draws on various OSW publications on the National Agenda for Women.)

One qualification is immediately necessary. It was an OSW initiative, taken in 1985, which paved the way for the emergence of domestic violence as a federal issue. In that year the office began a process of community consultation, designed to establish a National Agenda for Women, in order to provide an integrated plan for future government action on the status of women. It is significant that a preliminary statement made by the Prime Minister at the time did not envisage domestic violence as an area for further federal initiative, beyond the continued funding of refuges. The consultations occurred in 1986 and involved a series of meetings with women's groups all over the country, a call for submissions, of which over one thousand were received, and the widespread distribution of a questionnaire, to which over 13 500 women responded.

Out of this process, domestic violence emerged as a priority concern. Senator Susan Ryan, Minister assisting the Prime Minister on the status of women, made the following comment:

> The one [issue] that's come up [in the consulations] with an intensity that's surprised me has been the issue of violence against women ... The issues may relate to domestic violence or to community violence against women—rape and other crimes of a sexual nature. I must say I was shocked and really surprised that that issue has been dwelt on in every meeting. (*The Canberra Times* 19 April 86)

Nor was domestic violence simply a concern of self-identified feminists. The Country Women's Association, the National Council of Jewish Women and a variety of church groups all made submissions. Calls were made for more refuges, more vigorous action by the police and for educational campaigns. The National Council of Jewish Women suggested a campaign to 'promote awareness of the existence and dynamics of domestic violence—its causes, its nature and its extent'.

It was the depth of concern revealed in these consultations that led OSW to plan a three-year National Domestic Violence Education Campaign, starting in mid-1987, with a budget of $2.15 million. As a first step, a survey of community attitudes was conducted which revealed that one in five Australians thought violence by a man against his partner was acceptable in some circumstances, that almost half the respondents knew someone affected by domestic violence and that nearly a third believed that domestic violence was a private matter in which other people shouldn't interfere. Following the announcement of these results various educational activities were initiated, the most dramatic being the Domestic Violence Awareness Month in April 1989, launched by the Prime Minister and accompanied by an advertising blitz.

The national television and print media blitz was, however, only one aspect of OSW's educational campaign. A whole series of more finely targeted activities involving a more personal approach was also organised. In Domestic Violence Awareness Month more than 400 local community events were held around the country, an average of thirteen each day. At the same time OSW established an information network involving police, doctors, health workers, teachers, church workers and other service providers, and subsequently organised a variety of activities to promote concern about domestic violence in these groups. OSW also put together information kits aimed at particular populations—youth, rural women, Aboriginal women and so on—to be distributed through community groups having a particular interest in these populations. One of the highlights of this more specifically targeted campaign was a national training forum in Adelaide in April 1990 for people involved in the training of police, doctors, nurses and other service providers who come into contact with domestic violence. The basic aim was to encourage trainers to give greater attention to the issue of domestic violence in their training.

Research in the field of communications has consistently found that personal contact, not mass media advertising, is the best way to influence behaviour and opinions (Morehead and Penman, 1989: 15). It is clear that OSW's more finely targeted educational campaign, relying as it did on discussions, conferences and the personal transmission of information via community organisations, was carefully designed to maximise the impact of the message.

Our purpose at this point, however, is not to evaluate OSW's educational campaign, but to analyse it in terms of the role variability we have been discussing. The campaign was a direct response to requests from the wider women's movement. In this respect femocrats, at least at the federal level, have acted as agents of that movement rather than as initiators. By way of qualification, it must be noted that it was a femocrat initiative, the National Agenda for Women, which enabled the wider movement to express itself in the way it did. Furthermore, once the femocracy had been given its instructions, as it were, it again took the initiative in devising and implementing a sophisticated educational strategy. Thus, while the impetus for the OSW educational campaign came from the broader movement, the process by which the campaign emerged was an interactive and cooperative one, involving inputs and initiatives from both femocrats and women's groups outside the bureaucracy.

Although the educational campaign was of limited duration, OSW's involvement in the issue of domestic violence continues. The 1990 federal budget committed $1.35 million over three years to establish a National Committee on Violence Against Women. The committee is to carry out further community education as well as have a policy and research role.

CONCLUSION

In this chapter we have found it helpful in understanding the femocrats' role to see them as acting both as agents and as initiators. On occasions, femocrats take initiatives which are largely independent of the broader women's movement, for instance, initiatives on how the femocrats are to organise themselves within the bureaucracy. At other times femocrats can be seen acting as the agents of the broader movement—in a sense, at its behest. In relation to domestic violence, femocrats have acted, on the whole, as agents. On the question of refuge funding they represented the interests of the refuges to government. As for the federal campaign against domestic violence, this too has been largely a response to the broader movement. It is clear that the dynamism of the movement against domestic violence has come from the refuge workers. Femocrats have played a vital support role. Again we stress that this is not to be read as belittling their involvement; it has of course been invaluable. It is the collaboration between women inside and outside the bureaucracy which has enabled the movement against domestic violence to make the progress it has.

In the chapter which follows we examine in detail the nature of this collaboration in a particular case—the establishment of a Domestic Violence Crisis Service in Canberra. We shall find that, although the relationship was not always harmonious, the initiatives of each group built on those of the other and the partnership which developed in this way was vital to the outcome.

4 The origins of the Domestic Violence Crisis Service

The Domestic Violence Crisis Service (DVCS) began operation in Canberra in April 1988. To understand its origins we must go back to the early 1980s. The story is a fascinating one, revealing a complex interplay of several social forces. Prominent among them are the two strands of the feminist movement which we have highlighted in this book—refuge workers and femocrats. But we shall also see that concern about domestic violence was by this time being expressed by other sections of the community. Our story is intimately bound up with the the issue of law reform, an aspect of social change which so far has not been emphasised. We begin, therefore, with a brief account of the law reform processes.

Perhaps the best known organs of law reform are the law reform commissions (Kirby, 1980; Ross, 1982). Such commissions consider various areas of law thought to be in need of reform and make recommendations to government. Government then considers the proposals and enacts them, as it sees fit. Law reform commissions date back to the nineteenth century, but the 1960s saw their rapid development throughout the countries of the British Commonwealth, starting in the UK in 1965. In Australia, the first of this new wave of commissions was established in 1967 in New South Wales, and in the next few years commissions were established in almost every state in Australia, culminating in an Australian Law Reform Commission in 1975. The first president of this federal commission, Mr Justice Kirby, has described this development as a 'movement', even a 'boom industry' (Kirby, 1980: 40,44). As we shall see, it is a movement which was much involved in the establishment of the DVCS.

But law reform commissions are by no means the only agencies of law reform. Occasionally reform may follow the report of a royal commission, and very commonly it follows the report of a governmental committee set up to inquire into a particular matter. Such committees have often been described as task forces. This diversity of approach is clearly evident in relation to domestic violence. Law reform in this area was initiated by task force reports in New South Wales in 1981 and Western Australia in 1986, by the report of a government-appointed legal consultant in Tasmania in 1983, and by a report by the Women's Policy Coordination Unit in the Premier's Department in Victoria in 1985. Only in the ACT has reform followed the report of a law reform commission.

LAW REFORM IN THE ACT

Domestic violence law reform was in the air in the ACT in the early 1980s. The New South Wales Task Force had reported in 1981, and its recommendations were enacted in 1983 in the Crimes (Domestic Violence) Amendment Act. Furthermore, the New South Wales Women's Coordination Unit had run a domestic violence awareness campaign (NSW Women's Advisory Council, 1987). These developments did not go unnoticed in Canberra.

In 1982, femocrats in the Office of the Status of Women recommended to the Liberal Attorney-General that a task force be set up to reform the law on domestic violence in the ACT. The recommendation was apparently shelved; certainly nothing had come of it by the time Labor came to power in March 1983.

Meanwhile, community concern was growing in Canberra, as is evident in the proceedings of the House of Assembly. (This was an elected body which advised the federal Minister for the Capital Territory on matters affecting the ACT. At the time Canberra had no self-government.) The Canberra Women's Refuge played a central role in promoting this concern; one of its workers, Robyn Walmsley, was also a member of the Assembly and regularly raised refuge issues in debates. Moreover, refuge funding requests were routinely dealt with by the Assembly and these were also occasions for debate about the problem of domestic violence.

On 16 November 1982 a Democrat member of the Assembly moved a motion asking the Assembly to set up an inquiry into the problem of domestic violence. After an extensive debate which drew heavily on the experiences of the refuge, the motion was passed. It looked, at this stage, as if law reform in the ACT might be initiated by a sub-committee of the House of Assembly. But this decision was quickly overtaken by events. In March 1983, the new Attorney-General was again considering the appointment of a federal government task force, presumably at the instigation of the Office of the Status of Women. The Assembly therefore decided, on 29 March 1983, to abandon its own investigation and to formally recommend to the Attorney-General that the task force be appointed as soon as possible and that it include a representative of the Assembly. On 24 October 1983 the Assembly was formally notified that the task force was to be set up and was advised that its composition and terms of reference would be a matter for negotiation between the Attorney-General's nominee to the task force and the Assembly's. It is interesting that in subsequent correspondence, the Attorney-General spoke of the proposal as having come from the House of Assembly and it was thereafter regarded as an Assemby initiative. Be that as it may, it now appeared that law reform would follow the task force route, as it had in New South Wales.

But again, events took a different direction. To understand this new direction we must be aware of a further development which occurred at this time in what we described earlier as the law reform movement. (The following account draws on the annual reports of the Australian Law Reform Commission.) In August 1983 the Australian Law Reform Commission which, surprisingly, is located in Sydney, opened a branch office in Canberra, under the leadership of Professor David Hambly. Hambly was at the time working virtually full time on a report on the law of matrimonial property. This was a national matter. But he was expected also to be responsible for a second area of work, the Labor government's new Community Law Reform Project, the aim of which was to make law reform more responsive to local community needs. The idea, borrowed from the New South Wales Law Reform Commission, was that the Commission should compile a register of law reform suggestions from individuals in the community. Many of these, it was hoped, would lead to small scale, self-contained projects which the Commission could deal with quickly, without the need for an extensive inquiry. Projects would still need to be authorised by the Attorney-General, but the initiative would now come from the community and the Commission, rather than from the government. In this way, it was hoped, the processes of law reform might be speeded up. At the end of 1983 an ANU law lecturer, Nick Seddon, was appointed temporarily to the Commission to assist specifically with the Community Law Reform Project.

Hambly wrote to various community organisations for suggestions and by close of the year a number had been received, although none, it seems, concerned domestic violence. Nevertheless, Hambly was disposed to give domestic violence a high priority. He had taught family law for years and was aware of the inadequacies of the law in this respect. Moreover, he was a member of the Family Law Council of Australia, a national body set up by the federal government to monitor the operation of the Family Law

Act. At the time the council's annual reports were commenting regularly on the problem of domestic violence, and in 1980, following representations from the National Women's Advisory Council and members of the Hobart Women's Refuge, the council decided to undertake a major examination of the issue. Furthermore, one of the council's members was also a member of the New South Wales Task Force on domestic violence which recommended law reform in that state in 1981. Hambly was much influenced by his experiences on the council and saw his new appointment as an opportunity to do something about domestic violence in the ACT. Seddon, who had worked in the Community Legal Service and edited the ACT *Legal Resources Book,* was also very aware of the need for law reform in relation to domestic violence. By the end of 1983, therefore, two routes to law reform in this area were potentially available: a federal government task force and an inquiry by the Australian Law Reform Commission under its Community Law Reform Project.

Meanwhile, the Attorney-General's Department was negotiating with the Department of Territories and Local Government about who should provide the resources for the proposed task force. Neither department appeared willing to take on the administrative responsibility (House of Assembly, Hansard, 18 June 1984). Aware of this impasse, the Law Reform Commission offered to do the job, and the Attorney-General gratefully accepted. On 1 June 1984 he issued the Commission with a reference, that is, formal instructions to carry out the inquiry, and announced that the task force would no longer be proceeded with. The path to law reform had finally been settled.

The Commission worked fast. Within weeks Seddon was drafting a discussion paper and seeking input from community representatives. During this period, eight people were formally appointed consultants to the Commission, among them, the director of the Canberra Marriage Counselling Service, a representative of the OSW and a representative of the House of Assembly who had also been a refuge worker. Two other refuge workers also participated in consultations at this stage and one of them was subseqently formally appointed a consultant. Four years later, both were to get jobs with the crisis service. Seddon's paper was finalised and issued as a formal discussion paper by the Commission in October 1984.

The Commission also agreed to a suggestion to conduct a phone-in, in conjunction with the Australian Institute of Criminology and the Capital Territory Health Commission, to ascertain something of the experience of victims of violence in the ACT. The phone-in, timed to coincide with the release of the discussion paper, was held during the second week of October, and an extensive media campaign was conducted inviting victims to call. About 120 people responded and the results are analysed in the Commission's final report.

A CRISIS SERVICE PROPOSAL

The discussion paper of October 1984 contained many of the proposals for law reform which appeared in the final report in 1986. They were similar to the reforms occurring in other states and we shall reserve discussion of them for later chapters. What is of interest here is the proposal for the establishment of a crisis service contained in the paper. It was described as follows:

> What is envisaged here is a crisis intervention unit which, in addition to providing crisis intervention services, is a nerve-centre for information and referral. The unit would have to operate 24 hours a day and would be staffed by professional welfare workers. It would be linked to the police radio telephone system and have its own mobile cars with radio telephones. They would be responsible for arranging emergency accommodation and for short-term support and counselling. They would then be responsible for taking the victim or the couple to other appropriate agencies for longer term management of their problems. The unit would be a central point to which other people such as health workers or lawyers could refer domestic violence victims.
>
> The attackers, too, could use the unit for advice and referral. In many cases, the unit would initiate contact with the attacker.
>
> The workers in the unit would be available to go out to people's homes either at the request of the victim, the attacker or the police.
>
> Such a unit has been operating successfully and effectively in South Australia. It deals with many types of crises, not just domestic violence.
>
> In summary, it is submitted that a 24-hour domestic violence unit, together with effective publicity, is an indispensable and vital part of the strategy for dealing with domestic violence. The South Australian crisis intervention unit is regarded by workers in the field as the single most effective measure that has been adopted to deal with domestic violence ...

It is worth noting that this detailed description was not present in an earlier draft of the discussion paper. The draft speaks more generally of a centralised domestic violence unit, whose role is to provide accommodation services and counselling. It makes no mention of intervention at the scene of the crisis. Nor is there any mention of the South Australian model. What we wish to stress is that it was the community consultation process which took place during the drafting of the paper which ensured that the final version contained a clear proposal for a crisis intervention service. Seddon held a series of meetings with community representatives at which it was argued that the ACT should have a crisis service similar to the the one in South Australia. Indeed, it was specifically suggested by at least one consultant that the way this service operated should be sketched in the final version of the discussion paper. And that is exactly what was done. (For a full description of the South Australian Crisis Care Unit see Paterson, 1980.)

CONCURRENT INITIATIVES

The input made by the Commission's consultants was a reflection of a broader community concern about domestic violence which was being expressed at the time. The national conference of Marriage Guidance Councils, held in Canberra in April 1984, took domestic violence as its theme and was addressed by the Director of the South Australian Spouse Abuse Intervention Project (another South Australian innovation, not connected with the Crisis Care Unit). It was to be expected, therefore, that the Director of the Canberra Marriage Counselling Service, Malise Arnstein, would play an influential role in the Law Reform Commission consultations, as indeed she did.

Another Canberra organisation which was expressing concern about domestic violence at the time was the Capital Territory Health Commission, later the ACT Health Authority. The Commission had responsibilty for a wide range of community health and social services and the workers in these services were regularly confronted by instances of violence in families. Representatives of the Health Commission attended the meetings called by the Law Reform Commissioner to discuss his drafts and were also involved, as mentioned earlier, in organising the phone-in. In addition, the Health Commission held an extended series of workshops on domestic violence for its health care workers. The first two, in April and June 1985, were held in Canberra and Adelaide respectively, the latter to study South Australia's innovative responses to the problem. A third workshop took place in November. Two further workshop/conferences were held in 1986. This activity on the part of the Health Authority was an important part of the groundswell which culminated in the establishment of the DVCS.

This groundswell is most clearly manifested by an extraordinary organisation which sprang to life after the first two Health Authority workshops in 1985. Calling itself the Domestic Violence Interagency (DVIA), it brought together all the organisations in Canberra with an interest in the issue. Over the the next three years the DVIA met almost monthly to exchange information, comment publicly on developments and lobby for change. Much of its effort, as we shall shortly see, was directed towards the establishment of a crisis service. At its peak, the DVIA drew more than 30 people to its meetings and over its three-year life nearly 50 agencies and community groups were represented. We list them here, to convey some idea of the strength of this organisation and the breadth of community concern:

The Law Reform Commission
Australian Federal Police
City Counselling Unit, ACTHA
CARE (Credit and Debt Counselling)
Family Court Counselling
Canberra Marriage Counselling
Lifeline Telephone Counselling Service
Vietnam Veterans Counselling Service
Belconnen Community Service
Tuggeronong Community Service
Woden Community Service
Weston Creek Community Service
Melba Neighbourhood Centre
ACT Health Authority—Mental Health Branch
ACT Health Authority—Health Promotion Branch
ACT Health Authority—Policy and Planning Section
Queanbeyan Community Health Centre
Kambah Health Centre
Melba Health Centre
Family Planning Association
ACT Women's Unit
Women's Shopfront
Migrant Resource Centre
Queanbeyan Multi-Lingual Centre
Migrant Welfare, Dept of Immigration and Ethnic Affairs
Catholic Social Services
St Saviour's Neighbourhood Centre, Goulburn
Monica House—St Vincent de Paul
Doris Women's Refuge
Canberra Women's Refuge
Queanbeyan Women's Refuge
The Incest Centre
Caroline Chisolm Refuge
John Langmore's Office (MHR for Fraser)
Ros Kelly's Office (MHR for Canberra)
Senator Susan Ryan's Office
Challenge
Navy—Social Work

Army Community Services
Dept of Trade
Attorney-General's Department
Dept of Youth and Community Services—Queanbeyan
Royal Canberra Hospital
Woden Valley Hospital
Parent Support Service
Welfare Branch—Dept of the Capital Territory
Housing Branch—Dept of the Capital Territory
Alcohol and Drug Service Community Unit

Yet another expression of community concern at the time was the domestic violence conference held by the Australian Institute of Criminology in November 1985. This was the largest conference ever hosted by the Institute and was a year in planning. Community groups provided input at the planning stage and lobbied for the conference to emphasise the experience of people working directly with domestic violence. In the event, the conference was a largely academic affair, and refuge and other community workers demonstrated in protest, generating a great deal of publicity in the process. The DVIA wrote a long letter of protest to the Attorney-General about the conduct of the conference. Despite the controversy, or perhaps because of it, the conference served to focus community attention on domestic violence in an almost unprecedented way.

THE FINAL LAW REFORM REPORT

In December 1985 Seddon presented a summary of the Law Reform Commission's final report to the DVIA, and the report itself became available in March 1986. In addition to input from its consultants, the Commission acknowledged submissions from 30 different organisations and individuals.

Apart from its recommendation for a crisis service, which we shall address shortly, the report contained a series of specific recommendations for law reform. The Attorney-General's Department acted on these latter recommendations without delay and the new law came into effect in October 1986.

The Department's quick response in this respect is attributable to the deep concern aroused in the community by a tragedy which occurred in Canberra in February, 1986. Following the breakup of a de facto marriage, a man shot dead his ex-partner and both her parents, shot the woman's brother, leaving him permanently brain-damaged and, finally, killed himself. Two days before the killings the woman had asked the Magistrates Court to protect her, and a process was set in motion which might have led, days later, to the granting of a keep the peace order. It is unlikely that any legislation could have averted this tragedy, but the ineffectiveness of the court's response led to a public outcry and a demand that the law be reformed without delay.

The Canberra Times fuelled this demand by publishing a picture of the seriously injured boy being carried, unconscious, from the scene of the murders. The picture shocked many Canberra residents who wrote to the paper complaining about its sensationalism. The editor responded that his purpose was to draw attention to the problem of domestic violence. He wrote:

> *The Canberra Times* can publish endless editorials and reports of conferences with very little effect. The photograph drew far more concern and attention. It is sad that it takes this sort of tragedy (and wide publication of it) to do it ... If the publication of the photo moves a few people in power to help protect the victims of domestic violence, then it would have achieved its purpose. (15 February 1986)

There is no doubt that these events assured the rapid implementation of the legislative reforms recommended in the report.

More importantly for present purposes, the report also included a recommendation for the establishment of a so-called 'domestic violence unit'. It rejected a suggestion which had been made in one submission that the unit should be set up within the police force and suggested, instead, that it be established by the Department of the Capital Territory, in conjunction with the ACT Health Authority. In some ways, however, the final report retreated from the discussion paper recommendation. It mentioned the South Australian crisis intervention unit but noted that this dealt with all types of crises, not just domestic violence. It noted that, being a 24-hour service, the Adelaide unit was very costly and that such a unit would be too expensive for the ACT. In contrast to the earlier discussion paper, the report recommended a 9-to-5 service with a telephone answering machine for after-hours callers. There was no mention of mobile crisis teams. Nor was there any expectation that workers would attend 'domestics' with the police, but rather that police would refer victims and attackers to the unit, either orally or by giving them a pamphlet. The proposed service, then, was no longer the 'crisis intervention unit' envisaged in the original discussion paper. Strangely, this retreat from the original proposal passed without comment at the time.

THE REFUGE RESPONSE

In May 1986 the DVIA discussed the Law Reform Commission

report at length. The discussion focused on a long list of comments prepared by the Canberra Women's Refuge collective and was led by Dennise Simpson, the refuge representative. Over the next two years Dennise Simpson was to be a hard working member of every committee involved in the creation of the crisis service (except for a purely governmental committee). In due course she was employed by the crisis service, and in recognition of her long involvement with the issue she was appointed to a national task force on domestic violence in 1988. In late 1990 she was appointed coordinator of the crisis service following the resignation of its first coordinator.

In relation to the proposed unit the refuge expressed the following concerns:

1 The independence of the unit was vital and this meant that it should not be established within a government department.
2 It was better to have the unit staffed by people with work experience in the field of domestic violence, and not necessarily by 'professionals' or 'experts', as envisaged in the report.
3 It was preferable that the staff be all female, rather than mixed, as was the case with some crisis units interstate.
4 It was not appropriate that attackers come for help to a unit assisting victims.

These ideas constituted a real challenge to the spirit of the report, for what the refuge had in mind was a *feminist* crisis service, something which the report implicitly rejected. A blueprint for such a service had been clearly articulated in 1983 by Jocelynne Scutt in her book, *Even in the Best of Homes.* It had not, however, influenced the Commission's thinking. Scutt wrote as follows:

> Funds should be provided for teams of trouble shooters, feminists who, like women's refuge workers, are fully acquainted with the workings of the bureaucracy and of the court system. Whenever a woman calls and wants their help, the team would visit her, inform her of her rights, how to go about a legal clarification of her rights in the family property, how to gain sole custody of children, and if necessary, how to prevent her husband from continuing to abuse and harass her in her own home . . . Trouble shooters would assist women through the maze of relevant community welfare departments to discover what benefits are available to them for rent payments, or mortgage payments, electricity and rates payments, so the family home or lease could be kept on in their name. The team would talk with any woman who wished [it] about the nature of a society which placed her in a position of subservience to a man who took it upon himself to beat her regularly—or irregularly—until she could take it no more and begged—or demanded—help. (1983: 271–2)

It is appropriate, at this stage, to spell out more clearly the difference between a feminist crisis service and a non-feminist or orthodox service. An orthodox service is gender-blind, in the sense that it makes no *a priori* assumptions about the gender of victims. It does not assume that domestic violence is an expression of gender inequality, but rather an outcome of conflict, perhaps brought on by alcohol or stress. It presumes that a conflict-resolution strategy may be the appropriate response in many cases.

However, the most striking thing about the domestic violence which comes to the attention of the authorities is that it is almost always women who are the victims—over 95 per cent on many estimates (e.g. O'Donnell and Saville, 1982: 54). Moreover, it is almost always women who are in fear for their safety, not men. Men who call the police—and some do—do so not out of fear. (We will discuss this in greater detail in a later chapter.) The fact is that the refuges are crowded with women who have left home to escape violence, but we have never heard of a man leaving home for this reason.

None of the orthodox explanations of domestic violence—alcohol, stress, conflict—can explain this basic fact, that overwhelmingly it is women who are the victims. The one explanation which can is the feminist analysis, which sees domestic violence as largely an outcome of gender inequality, as an expression of male domination.

A feminist service would build systematically on this analysis. It would see its fundamental task as the empowerment of women, making them aware that they do not have to put up with violence, making them aware that there are other options. Naturally, such a service would be staffed by women.

We see, then, that in calling for a feminist service, the refuge workers were challenging the Law Reform Commission recommendation and indeed the South Australian model which so far had dominated the discussion. The odds against them were considerable on this issue but, as we shall see, they persisted, and it is a tribute to their commitment and powers of persuasion that the service finally established displayed many of the characteristics for which they had struggled.

A DVIA INITIATIVE

At its next meeting, in June 1986, the DVIA decided to set up a working party to look specifically at the issue of a crisis unit. It consisted of eight people, including the director of the Canberra Marriage Counselling Service, who served as convenor, the law reform commissioner and a representative of the women's refuge.

The working party met on several occasions, and issued a questionnaire to the 34 agencies at that time represented on the DVIA. It also read the WA Domestic Violence Task Force report which appeared in January 1986 and took particular note of its recommendation that a crisis unit, staffed by civilians, be established within the Police Department. The working party report was finalised in August. It recommended a unit attached to the police but staffed by civilians. The unit was to have mobile teams which would attend 'domestics' with the police. It was thus to be a true crisis intervention unit. It would also provide a telephone counselling and information service. The report suggested that the unit employ male and female workers, but it noted that some respondents to its survey had favoured women only teams. Thus, the working party ignored the Law Reform Commission suggestion of a 9-to-5 service in favour of a 24-hour crisis intervention approach. It did not, however, support the refuge position that the unit should be independent of government and staffed by women only.

But the DVIA had no budget of its own and was in no position to implement its proposal. Ultimately, the establishment of a crisis service was a matter for government, and it is here that femocrats played a crucial role.

THE GOVERNMENT RESPONSE

Following the appearance of the Law Reform Commission report, the Minister for Territories approved the establishment of a committee to consider the implementation of the non-legal recommendations of the report, most particularly, the recommendation for a domestic violence unit. This decision was based on a submission to the Minister from Linda Webb, a first assistant secretary in the department, reflecting advice received from the Women's Unit within the department. Thus women inside the bureaucracy were now playing their part. The implementation committee, with the women's advisor as its chair, was essentially an IDC (Inter-Departmental Committee), a ubiquitous feature of the Canberra bureaucracy. Its first meeting was in July 1986. It consisted of representatives from the following government agencies:

Women's Unit, Department of Territories
Welfare Services Branch, Department of Territories
Housing Branch, Department of Territories
ACT Health Authority
ACT Schools Authority

Australian Federal Police,
Magistrates Court, Attorney-General's Department

This group of government-sector agencies was to appear time and again on subsequent committees.

The creation of the new committee was announced to the DVIA at its August meeting. On the face of it there seemed to be substantial overlap between the functions of the implementation committee and the DVIA and the suggestion was made that it was perhaps time to disband the DVIA. The women's advisor, Ann Wentworth, a member of both bodies, argued strongly against this suggestion. She realised that the implementation committee would need strong community input and support if an appropriate service were to be established. She stressed that no proposals would be implemented without prior consultation with the DVIA. In the following months she adhered to this policy, scrupulously. Her view was that the DVIA was in a position to exert community pressure on the Minister in a way that the implementation committee was not. This quickly proved to be the case.

The implementation committee initially took the view that funding was not available for a 24-hour crisis intervention unit. It proposed, instead, a 9-to-5 telephone service to provide information and referral. The service would be staffed by a single worker. An important feature of this proposal was that it could be funded from the Department of Territories' existing budget, which the department agreed to do.

In October 1986 the implementation committee invited members of the DVIA and other interested individuals to a special meeting to present this proposal, among other things. The reaction was intense. Both at this special meeting and at the normal October meeting of the DVIA a few days later, the telephone counselling service was severely criticised as being totally inadequate. The DVIA issued a press release to this effect, emphasising the need for a crisis intervention unit. Moreover, at least one of its member organisations, the Marriage Counselling Service, wrote a strongly worded letter to the Minister attacking the proposed 'hotline' as a token step, quite incapable of dealing with the real problem. It emphasised that 'The weakest link in dealing with domestic violence is the gap between police attendance at the scene of a crisis and a referral to and follow up of victims and perpetrators with relevant services. There is a need for a 24 hour crisis service to attend family crises to fill this gap.' Clearly, the DVIA was performing the very role which the women's advisor had foreseen— maintaining the pressure for a fully-fledged crisis intervention service.

Despite the protest, the proposal for a telephone service went ahead, and perhaps because of it the department was now offering to provide two full-time workers rather than one. The real significance of the community protest, however, was that it sent a very clear message to government about the importance which the community attached to the establishment of a true crisis intervention unit.

Two months later, in December 1986, the Minister issued a press release announcing that the department would make a submission to federal Cabinet for a special budget allocation for a 24-hour crisis intervention service. It does not follow, of course, that the government's decision in this respect was simply a response to the community protest; departmental officers already had in mind the possibility of a budget submission. The decision would also have been influenced by a letter from the Attorney-General to the Minister in October urging the establishment of a crisis intervention unit 'as a matter of urgency'. But there can be little doubt that the community outcry strengthened the department's resolve to proceed in this way.

In November 1986, just prior to the ministerial press release, the women's advisor called a combined meeting of the DVIA and the implementation committee to announce this new initiative and sort out details of the telephone service. It would be her job to draft the submission. If it succeeded, the money would become available some time after the August 1987 budget announcement. The telephone service was now seen as an interim measure and it was even argued that one of its functions would be to generate statistics demonstrating the need for a crisis intervention unit. These could then be used in the budget submission. The meeting agreed on a management committee for the telephone service consisting of the membership of the inter-departmental implemenation committee, plus one community representative, chosen by the DVIA. The Minister accepted a recommendation to this effect and matters were now in the hands of this new committee. Having done its work, the implementation committee itself went into recess in December.

A COMMUNITY SERVICE?

A process was now in train which would lead in just over a year to the establishment of a full-scale crisis intervention service. But two fundamental issues were yet to be dealt with. First, there was the question of whether the new services would be located in the government or non-government sector, and, second, the question of whether the services would be in some sense feminist. These were overlapping but by no means identical questions.

Moreover, they were controversial questions. On one side of the debate were the police and the courts, who wanted any new service to be a part of government, and certainly not feminist in its philosophy. On the other side were the refuge workers and various community groups who wanted a feminist, non-government organisation.

To understand the way matters developed, we need to know a little more of the personal politics of the women's advisor, Ann Wentworth. She had previously worked for the ACT Council of Social Services, an association of non-governmental organisations, and she regarded herself as having 'come from the community'. She was strongly committed, therefore, to the view that the new service should be located in the community, that is, run by an organisation which was independent of government. Moreover, as a feminist, she espoused a patriarchal analysis of domestic violence. Thus, on many of the issues which came up for discussion, she and the refuge workers were in agreement. As we shall show in some detail, the way the crisis service eventually took shape owes much to this femocrat–refuge worker alliance.

It was clear that the ultimate resolution of these matters would be crucially affected by the composition of the decision-making committees formed along the way. Considered in this light, the composition of the new telephone service management committee was not at all promising, from the community perspective. All, bar the DVIA nominee, were drawn from the government sector.

However, at its first meeting, towards the end of December, the new committee agreed to a request from community groups that a second community representative be appointed. Finally, in March, the committee accepted a third, as an 'honorary member'. The balance was clearly shifting.

Despite this shift in the composition of the committee, the presumption at this stage was that the telephone workers would be employees of the Department of Territories and that the service would thus be in the government sector. The positions were advertised in January 1987, but a dispute then arose over their public service classification and whether the funding was really available. As a result, the whole process came to a standstill and was finally overtaken by other events.

BREAKTHOUGH

The bureaucratic delays being experienced over public service classification of the positions convinced doubters on the DVIA that the new telephone service should not be located in the government sector and the DVIA decided at its July meeting to lobby the government on this point. Accordingly, in mid-July the women's advisor took a delegation of three DVIA members, two of them refuge workers, to discuss the matter with senior officials of the Department of Territories. The DVIA representatives urged a community location, on the grounds that the new service needed to have maximum community acceptance. The officials agreed, but specified that in order to receive funding the controlling body needed to be accountable and incorporated and to have an appropriate management structure. This was a critical breakthrough for the advocates of the community view.

It is worth stressing that there was nothing inevitable about this outcome. Participants in these events speak of attending one meeting after another, without any clear understanding of what lay ahead. There was certainly continual pressure, particularly from the women's advisor and the community service and refuge workers on the DVIA, for maximum community say in the operation of the new service, but this did not translate automatically into a decision to locate the service in the non-government sector. Indeed, as we have seen, matters were proceeding on the assumption that the telephone service would be part of the Department of Territories, until the job classification dispute arose. It was thus essentially a chance event which enabled community pressure to be brought to bear decisively.

Following this breakthrough, the DVIA proposed that it should provide the management committee for the new community-based telephone service and this proposal was accepted by the department. The committee elected by the DVIA consisted of four refuge workers and four other community representatives sympathetic to the refuge position. All four refuge women were subsequently successful applicants for jobs with the crisis service.

The new management committee rapidly drew up a statement of aims and objectives for the telephone service which was thoroughly feminist in its philosophy. Amongst these aims were the following:

1 to change the inherent power difference between men and women which creates and perpetuates domestic violence; and
2 to raise awareness of the high incidence of domestic violence [and] the patriarchal social relations from which domestic violence is created and maintained.

In addition, the document emphasised the importance of sensitivity to the needs of women from different class and ethnic backgrounds, and specified that one of the service's aims was 'to actively confront racism, sexism and class oppression on the committee'.

The ideals and commitments of the refuge workers were clearly embodied in these aims and objectives. Their tenacity and their dedication to a feminist vision were finally achieving results. Not surprisingly, the two workers employed by the new committee had both worked in refuges. The telephone service commenced operation in November, but events were moving so quickly that it was absorbed into the crisis service soon after it began.

THE CRISIS SERVICE TAKES SHAPE

Meanwhile, the submission for funding for a full-scale crisis service had been successful. This was really a double success. First, the Department of Territories had agreed that the proposal merited its strong support and had given it a top ranking on its list of requests. Secondly, the proposal was looked upon favourably by the federal government's expenditure review committee and by Cabinet. By contrast, most of the funding submissions made by Territories were knocked back in the budget review process. Domestic violence was clearly given a high priority by the government, no doubt as a result of the findings generated by the Office of the Status of Women in 1986 on the extent of concern among women across the country. The submission's prospects were also enhanced when the idea of a crisis intervention service was endorsed in December 1986 by a special meeting of heads of government departments called to consider the National Agenda for Women. Finally, Canberra's multiple murder of early 1986 was probably still in people's minds. So it was that in September 1987 the government announced that a 24-hour-a-day, seven-day-a-week service would be established.

The women's advisor quickly set about constituting an interim management committee. In line with the earlier decisions the new service was to be located in the non-government sector and would need to be set up as an incorporated body with a constitution and a management committee. Department of Territories, now the ACT Administration, was keen that the government should retain a strong say in the operation of the service and decided that the interim management committee should consist of the original government-sector implementation committee, plus five community representatives. Accordingly, the women's advisor called a meeting of all DVIA members in September to elect the community representatives. Two women with refuge experience were among those chosen. A third was later invited to join the committee in her capacity as telephone service worker.

At its first meeting, in September 1987, the interim management committee made various decisions concerning the structure of the incorporated community organisation which would ultimately run the crisis service. In particular, it was decided that the permanent management/executive committee would consist of six official government representatives, six elected community representatives, and a representative of the staff.

Perhaps the most momentous decision made by the interim committee concerned the objectives for what was now to be called the Domestic Violence Crisis Service (DVCS). Three different sets of objectives were prepared for discussion, one of them strongly feminist in tone, taken from the aims and objectives of the telephone service. Amongst these aims were the following:

1   to change the inherent power difference between women and men which creates and perpetuates domestic violence;
2   to work towards the empowerment of all women and children; and
3   in cooperation with the police and other relevant agencies, to work towards the elimination of violence in interpersonal relationships.

Given the makeup of the committee, these were highly controversial aims. Small committees normally operate by consensus, but no consensus was possible on these objectives; they were put to the vote, one by one. Each was passed by a majority of one. On the whole, the government representatives opposed the proposed feminist aims and the community supported them, the women's advisor voting mostly with the community. The crisis service now had a feminist philosophy written into its very constitution. Again there was nothing inevitable about this outcome. As we have seen, the matter was touch and go, and the importance of previous decisions about the composition of the committee was now apparent.

The decision to adopt feminist objectives had immediate repercussions. The police representative wrote a formal letter, marked 'urgent', to the women's advisor, asking for the matter to be reconsidered. Canberra's chief magistrate also objected in a letter to the committee. He argued that if the court, through its representation on the management committee of the DVCS, was associated with feminist objectives, it might be seen as biased in favour of women in applications for domestic violence orders. However, the committee stood firm and politely rejected these representations. As a result, the chief magistrate declined to nominate a court representative to the permanent management committee, which met first in February 1988. He maintained his stance, despite a visit by a delegation from the committee, and the position set aside in the constitution for a court appointee is still vacant at the time of writing.

In January 1988 a public meeting was called to elect community representatives to the permanent management committee. Of the six elected, two were refuge workers. It had been agreed that the two telephone workers would automatically be given jobs as crisis workers once the new service was established, and so one of them immediately assumed the position of staff representative on the new permanent committee. Thus there were again three refuge workers involved as the permanent committee began its work.

THE QUESTION OF HIERARCHY

Throughout this period the three refuge workers were active on sub-committees, designing a ten-day training package for the workers once appointed, preparing cost statements and, most importantly, drawing up duty statements and selection criteria for the crisis workers and the coordinator. The work of this last sub-committee would have enormous significance for the way in which the crisis service operated and it is not surprising, therefore, given their interest in the service, that refuge workers held two of the four positions on this sub-committee.

Having worked in collectives, the refuge workers were philosophically opposed to the idea that the coordinator should exercise any power over other members of the crisis service. They had not been able to prevent the creation of a coordinator position in the constitution, although they had succeeded in having the position designated 'coordinator' and not 'director', as was the case in certain other constitutions on which the DVCS constitution was modelled. This was clearly more than a mere semantic difference. In drawing up the duty statements, therefore, they were interested in maximising the autonomy of the workers and creating as egalitarian a working environment as possible, within the limits imposed by the constitution. If the workers were to be empowering others, they needed to work in an environment which empowered them. The implications of this philosophy for the way the service was to operate will be dealt with in the next chapter.

CONCLUSION

The route leading to the establishment of the DVCS in Canberra was long and tortuous. We have seen, though, that the process was driven, from beginning to end, by community pressure. The most striking manifestation of this was the DVIA, a community-based organisation which gave expression to community views throughout the period.

As part of this general thrust, three more specific forces were at work: law reform, the femocrats and the refuge movement. Law reform was the starting point and generated the first specific recommendation for a crisis service. But it is important to recognise that law reform was not a process independent of the community. Pressure for reform was growing in the early 1980s and it was virtually inevitable that one or other of the possible routes to law reform would be followed. The one actually chosen was, to some extent, fortuitious.

Once the recommendation had emerged from the Law Reform Commission report and onto the government's agenda, the role of women in the bureaucracy was vital to the outcome. The proposal was supported by a very highly placed female bureaucrat, while the women's advisor pushed it through committee after committee, striving always for maximum community input. And the DVIA provided her with this input. The importance of refuge workers is evident throughout. Their vision of a feminist crisis service and their presence on all the committees formed along the way were essential features of the process.

We see, then, that both strands of the women's movement highlighted in this book, the femocracy and the refuge movement, played central roles in the establishment of the DVCS. The two groups did not always work together harmoniously, but it is clear that it was a *partnership* between the two which determined the outcome.

And what was the outcome? A crisis intervention service unique in Australia. The DVCS is located in the non-government sector, unlike any other in Australia, and it has a clearly specified feminist philosophy, unlike any other in Australia.

Finally, we should repeat that there was nothing inevitable about this outcome. Given community concern about domestic violence, it was probably inevitable that some form of crisis service would be established. After all, this has happened in almost every state of Australia. But there was nothing inevitable about its community location or its feminist philosophy. This was the particular achievement of the women's movement in Canberra, an achievement for which the femocrat–refuge worker partnership was vital.

5 The crisis service as an organisational hybrid

In the last chapter we recounted the struggle over the organisational form of the proposed crisis service. On the one hand were the bureaucrats and law enforcement authorities wanting a conventional bureaucratic hierarchy, preferably attached to an existing governmental organisation. On the other were the community groups, in particular the refuge workers, wanting a collective form, independent of government. The community groups were successful in achieving a community-based organisation, but bureaucratic interests were largely successful on the question of hierarchy. The DVCS was set up with a theoretically all-powerful committee of management, a coordinator, responsible for the day-to-day affairs of the service, and some twelve crisis workers, answerable to the committee. But despite this hierarchical structure, the service operates in some respects almost as if it were a collective. Indeed, one of its workers has described it as a 'Clayton's collective, the collective you have when you're not having a collective'. It is for this reason we regard it as a hybrid form of organisation.

In this chapter we shall argue that the hybrid nature of the DVCS has the potential to get the best out of both the collective and hierarchical organisational forms. On the one hand it has the potential to provide a non-alienating work environment for its employees. On the other, the DVCS satisfies the needs of other organisations (government departments, the police etc.) by operating with an identifiable spokesperson who is also seen to be accountable for DVCS activity. The existence of a single person who represents the service to outsiders has assisted its rapid acceptance by the wider community. This acceptance has also depended, of course, on the demonstrated expertise of the crisis workers themselves.

THE SOURCES OF THE HYBRID FORM

The hybrid form of the DVCS is, in part, a result of the compromise struck between community groups and officials over the form the service should take. Traces of this compromise can be seen in the documents setting up the service. The constitution sets up an executive or management committee, composed of community and government representatives and charges it with the responsibility of the running of the service. Nowhere in the constitution are these powers formally delegated to the coordinator. Indeed the role of the coordinator is quite unspecified. There is thus no basis in the constitution for the coordinator to exercise any authority over other employees. This is not simply a drafting oversight, but a result of the influence of refuge workers on the committee which drafted the constitution. They were committed to the view that the values implicit in hierarchies, in particular, the assumed right of some to exercise power over others, tended to reproduce the very dynamics of the violent relationships to which they were opposed. As we shall show in some detail in a later chapter, it is the right which some men assume to exercise power over their female partners which is the root cause of domestic violence.

This same concern was also evident in the makeup of the original management committee. A staff representative with full voting rights was to be a member, but there was no place for the coordinator. When the service began operation this turned out to be an impractical arrangement, and it was decided to include the coordinator on the committee, but without voting rights.

A further document developed in the initial stages sets out the terms and conditions of employment of the crisis workers. It specifies the coordinator as being responsible for various administrative matters, such as record keeping and authorisation of leave. The coordinator is empowered to make recommendations to the management committee on matters of hiring, but has no privileged role in relation to firing; this is a matter for the committee, acting on the advice of its personnel and disputes sub-committee. There is thus very little power formally vested in the coordinator's position when it comes to dealing with staff.

Finally, while the job specification for the coordinator says that the coordinator is answerable to the management committee, that of the crisis workers says nothing about to whom they are answerable.

It is clear from this account that those responsible for drafting these various documents were seeking to maximise worker autonomy and minimise the potential for the disempowerment of workers inherent in hierarchical forms of organisation. The 'boss' was to be a token boss only, and not in a position to disempower the workers.

Quite apart from these formal considerations, a major factor which has contributed to the service's quasi-collective method of operation is the background of the crisis workers. Nine of the thirteen initially offered jobs as crisis workers had worked previously in collectives, mostly refuges. These workers were strongly committed to collective principles and sought to apply them in their new job. It should be noted that the preponderance of ex-refuge workers in the service is not a result of any deliberate policy on the part of the selection committee. The committee consisted of one former refuge worker, two community workers—all three female—and a male social worker from the Health Authority. The fact is that in terms of their expertise, enthusiasm, commitment and experience, refuge workers were clearly the best qualified for the job.

QUASI-COLLECTIVE FUNCTIONING

The service operates from rented accommodation whose location is kept secret so as to minimise the potential for harassment by aggrieved perpetrators of violence. Indeed, the intention is that the location be changed from time to time to maintain security. The quasi-collective nature of the service was symbolised by the office layout at its first location. The floor space was not sub-divided in any way, and the coordinator's desk was just one of several in the room. In contrast to a conventional hierarchical organisation, the coordinator thus had no privileges or privacy and indeed the practice was that anything on her desk might be read by any worker, the principle being that no-one in the work group should have exclusive access to information. It is well known, after all, that control over information is one of the fundamental techniques by which power is exercised, and there is a commitment on the part of all concerned that the coordinator should not be in a position to exercise power over the staff.

The policy is that all important decisions affecting the service are made, not by the coordinator, but by the staff, including the coordinator, at regular monthly meetings. Issues such as the structure of shifts, new DVCS initiatives, and personnel matters are debated at these meetings and the coordinator is not in a position to determine the outcome. Decisions are taken sometimes by consensus and sometimes by vote and the coordinator can easily be overruled or even find herself in a minority of one. These decision-making processes have enabled workers to participate in management to a far greater extent than occurs in most organisations.

On personnel matters the staff are particularly concerned to protect the rights of individual workers. In most hierarchical organisations, when an employee is performing inadequately it is the responsibility of the supervisor to take action, be it remedial or disciplinary. In the case of the DVCS it would be the responsibility of the staff group. This policy would be implemented in ways characteristic of collectives. In theory, all discussions about the staff member concerned would have to take place in her presence. This is a difficult principle to live by, but it reflects a commitment to open and accountable decision making. Furthermore, staff would not be prepared to take action in relation to the inadequate performance of a co-worker unless they had had personal experience of it. There would be an unwillingness to rely on reports of others in such matters. This policy stems from a belief that group members should be as careful of one another's interests as circumstances allow.

While such policies serve to protect the rights of workers they also mean that it would be difficult to take remedial action in the event of inadequate performance. Of course there is nothing unique to this organisational form about this problem. It is a well known principle of conventional hierarchical organisations, at least those where there is some security of tenure, that people rise to their level of incompetence and remain there, performing inadequately, for long periods of time. It is perhaps only in hierarchies in the private sector that inadequate performance can be dealt with swiftly.

Although the DVCS is, we have argued, a quasi-collective, there are important features of the task performed by the DVCS which make it impossible for it to operate, even internally, in quite the way that other feminist collectives often do. A common refuge pattern is to employ certain workers for the first half of the week and another group for the second half, both groups working on Wednesday. The whole of Wednesday is set aside for meetings of the collective. The phone may be diverted to an answering machine or a relief worker hired to avoid interruptions and matters are talked out until consensus is achieved. The frequency and intensity of these meetings is essential for the successful operation of the collective mode of organisation.

In the case of the DVCS, the shift work nature of the job means that meetings of the whole staff must be more infrequent. There are three shifts a day, seven days a week, and at any one time there will be only one, or possibly two pairs of workers on duty. Any given pair works a complicated shift pattern of three days on, three off and six on, six off. In these circumstances, it is useful to have a coordinator working normal office hours to provide continuity and indeed coordination. This feature of the DVCS, regardless of any other, ensures that the coordinator has inevitably taken on a day-to-day decision-making role, in consultation with the staff on duty, not found in a fully fledged collective. Furthermore, the entire staff can only meet as a group if relief staff are hired for the duration of the meeting. This places a limit on the frequency and duration of staff meetings and thus a further limit on pure collective functioning.

THE COORDINATOR AND THE WIDER CONTEXT

In contrast to its internal functioning, the DVCS operates as a more conventional hierarchical organisation in the way it relates to the outside world. People outside the DVCS assume the coordinator to be the person 'in charge'. An external evaluation of the service is worth quoting at some length on this point:

> The DVCS is an agency which has to work within the wider context of all community services in Canberra. It has to relate to the media, police, legal area etc. To do this effectively its structure was set down by those who developed the concept and won funding as a hierarchy, in line with most other agencies in Canberra.
>
> This, according to all the respondents (from external agencies interviewed by the evaluator) except those from the refuges, has been its greatest strength. The reason given was its recognisable structure within which a person (coordinator) can make decisions on behalf of the agency efficiently and on-the-spot when needed. This was seen as important at inter-agency meetings and discussions. Although a number of other structures were possible, the only one mentioned by the other agencies was that of a collective. Generally a collective structure was seen as inefficient in decision making from their various points of view and most said that they would have had difficulty working with the DVCS if they had developed a collective structure. (Kelly, 1989: 45)

One of the most significant examples of the role played by the coordinator outside the service is in relations with police. Crisis workers work closely with the police and, as will be discussed more fully in a later chapter, there is considerable potential for friction and misunderstanding between the two groups at the crisis scene. Accordingly, an agreement worked out between the police and the DVCS prohibits either side from criticising the other at the time and specifies that such criticisms are to be dealt with in discussions between the coordinator and senior police. To facilitate communication at this level, regular meetings were instituted between the coordinator and the commanders of Canberra's three police stations. This procedure has been quite successful and many of the problems which arise between police and crisis workers are dealt with in this way. This rapport between the DVCS and senior police, despite widely differing philosophies and work practices, is in part attributable to the role played by the coordinator. These police have grown to feel comfortable with the DVCS because, as one police commander observed, it has a 'recognisable organisational structure with a person with a name and title as a contact rather than an agency name as a contact' (Kelly, 1989: 47). It is also the case that, over time, police have dropped some of their suspicion and learnt to trust and respect the crisis workers because of the way they do their job.

A second matter for which the existence of a single representative of the DVCS has been useful is funding. As mentioned in chapter 2, collectives are viewed with some caution by funding bodies because they are perceived to be insufficiently accountable for the money they receive. The DVCS was set up as a hierarchy to overcome precisely this problem. The structure of the DVCS has meant that in practice the coordinator is accountable, and she is seen as such outside the service. This has helped engender confidence in the service on the part of bureaucrats responsible for funding. Along with the demonstrated competence of crisis workers, this has been critical in maintaining the relatively high level of funding the service enjoys in comparison with other community groups.

A final example concerns relationships with the welfare section of the Territory government over emergency accommodation. When a woman needs to be removed immediately from a violent situation, the DVCS would normally seek to place her in a refuge. Should the refuges be full, the government department concerned may agree to pay for the women and her children to be accommodated in a motel, provided it is convinced that no other options are available. It is clearly impracticable for bureaucrats to be involved in such a decision in an after-hours emergency situation. And so, in part because of the demonstrated expertise of the crisis workers, and in part because there is a coordinator responsible, the department has agreed to delegate the decision to the DVCS in these circumstances.

It is clear, then, that the acceptance of the service by other agencies and its ability to integrate its operations with those of other agencies concerned with domestic violence has been made easier by the existence of a coordinator who functions for outsiders as the person 'in charge' of the DVCS. In this respect, the service has benefited from the hierarchical component of its organisational structure.

These considerations lead us to disagree with a suggestion made in a far-sighted article by Smith (1985: 61). In a discussion of how a feminist service such as the DVCS might operate, she writes as follows:

While this form of interventionary service could not operate as a collective in the same manner as a women's refuge, there need be no necessary establishment of a hierarchy within the service itself. As a collective, all workers, by virtue of their employment and not on the basis of their experience in the field, would be equally responsible for the operations of the service. Regular meetings and the institutionalised distribution of information ensures the equal participation of workers even where their experiences are irrelevant to their role in decision-making.

So far, so good. But she goes on:

For the purposes of contact with other agencies, a contact person could be determined on a rotational basis. This would be intended to extend and maintain the capacities of all workers within the service. Where all workers are cognizant of the practices of the services there will be no difficulty in maintaining contact with other agencies, whose concern is with an informed, rather than familiar, contact.

The experience of the DVCS suggests that outside agencies feel more comfortable if the person with whom they have contact is both informed *and* familiar. A rotating coordinator would preclude this familiarity. It would, moreover, destroy the sense which outsiders have that there is an identifiable person who is in some way accountable. In our view, a rotating coordinator would make relationships with outside agencies far more problematic. In the case of a women's refuge, which has only intermittent contact with the police, a rotating coordinator may function well, but in the case of the DVCS, which every day has multiple contact at varying levels within the police hierarchy, for instance, the continuity provided by a single coordinator is vital.

REFLECTIONS

We have shown in this chapter that the DVCS is an organisational hybrid, displaying features of both collective and hierarchical organisation. These are essentially incompatible organisational principles. Such an organisational form, therefore, embodies certain tensions. The point is that no group of workers with collective ideals can be entirely happy to have a coordinator imposed upon them by a constitution over which they have no control. The effective functioning of the organisation therefore requires real compromises on the part of those involved and a commitment to working cooperatively.

The success of the form depends, furthermore, on a clear articulation of the role of the coordinator. If she is not a conventional director, what *are* her responsibilities and what *is* the extent of her authority? These are questions which have confronted the DVCS and which need to be answered with considerable clarity if the full potential of this organisational form is to be achieved.

Our account has shown how the hybrid organisational form of the DVCS was not a preconceived design but rather the somewhat unpredictable outcome of an extended political process. There is, however, as we have also shown, a certain logic to it, and it is noteworthy that there are other feminist-inspired organisations which have adopted similar hybrid forms. One of the best documented is Melbourne's Centre Against Sexual Assault (CASA).

Like the DVCS, CASA has a committee of management consisting of six community representatives and six public-sector representives, from the Royal Women's Hospital in CASA's case. It has a team of ten workers, including a coordinator, and runs in accordance with an explicit feminist philosophy. In particular this means a strong commitment to minimise hierarchy and to empower workers. The role of the coordinator is clearly specified. Most strikingly, she has no part in forward planning, that being the responsibility of a rotating sub-group of workers of which she is never a member.

CASA describes its approach in the following terms (Anderson and Dean, 1989):

> There appears to be a tradition of polarisation in the establishment of sexual assault services. Sexual assault services have been established either as hospital-based 'clinics' reflective of a medical-model approach to service structure and provision, or as 'grassroots' rape crisis centres encompassing a feminist collectivist philosophy and model of operation.
>
> At CASA House a 'third' model has been implemented in an attempt to offer an alternative to the false dichotomy of earlier service models.
>
> The uniqueness of the CASA House model lies in its capacity to affirm, promote and implement principles of feminist practice within the mainstream setting of an institutionalised, orthodox medical model.

It is clear that CASA's 'third' model is similar, in principle, to the 'hybrid' form of the DVCS. The details, of course, are different and, in particular, the role of the coordinator is differently specified. Each such organisation will necessarily strike its own particular compromise between the hierarchical and collective forms of organisation.

The hybrid form, we would argue, makes such organisations effective instruments for social change. The hierarchical framework enables them to work with other hierarchical organisations in a cooperative way, relatively free of the antagonisms which too often characterise relations between collectives and bureaucracies. On the other hand, the commitment to collective principles among the staff provides a work environment in which high levels of worker autonomy are possible. Staff empowered in this way are likely to have a profound effect in altering the attitudes and thinking of those who come in contact with them. For this reason the hybrid is, we believe, the organisational form best able to facilitate the quiet revolution on which services such as the DVCS are bent.

6   Delivering the service

The vision of a crisis service in the minds of those working for its establishment was that it be an agency for social change. The aim was not simply to stop the violence in particular crisis situations but rather to confront the fundamental power imbalance between men and women which is at the root of male violence. In this chapter we shall show how the DVCS is going about this task.

CRISIS INTERVENTION

Perhaps the single most important function of the DVCS is to attend domestic violence incidents with the police. Every time the police receive a report of violence occurring in a household they notify the DVCS and a team of two crisis workers is dispatched immediately to wait in the vicinity of the house in question. The patrol police who respond to the call are required to seek an invitation from any occupant of the household, normally the woman, for the crisis workers to enter, and this is forthcoming in the great majority of cases. Once the invitation is issued it is relaid to crisis workers waiting outside. The fact that the crisis team is already in the vicinity has enabled invitations to be responded to immediately and in fact makes it more likely that they will be forthcoming.

Police statistics show that prior to the establishment of the DVCS the police attended about 60 such calls a month. After two years of DVCS operation the monthly rate was 70. This presumably reflects the crisis intervention work of the DVCS which has helped increase awareness among women of the remedies available to them. It is no doubt also at least in part attributable to the educational activities of the DVCS, to be described later.

Although there are countless variations, the following would be a typical scene into which the crisis workers enter on their arrival. There is still violence in the atmosphere. There is a woman who has been beaten. Sometimes the injuries are obvious but very often the blows have been directed to parts of her body which do not reveal obvious bruising, or which are covered by clothing. She may

have been kicked in the back of the head or beaten about the ears
or punched in the stomach. She will be hurting physically, and very
distressed. There is the man who has beaten her. He will be self-
righteous. He will be concerned that the police hear his side of the
story, which will involve justification and excuses for his behaviour,
and he will not like the attention that the crisis workers give his
wife. He will be aggressive and his potential to be violent will be
obvious, yet his words will protest his innocence. He will grossly
understate his own violence, claiming that he did not do anything
to her, and he will claim wild exaggeration on her part. He will
loudly complain about the violation of his personal rights by the
police and the crisis workers and the intrusion on his property.
There may also be children, cowering in a corner, or waiting fearfully in another room.

The police investigate the story to establish what action they will
take. If they judge the matter to be serious enough, they may arrest
the perpetrator or take him in to the police station to sober up. But
it is unusual for him to be removed in this way. The crisis workers
speak with the victim of the violence or, if the offender is at all
receptive, one will talk with the offender and one with the victim.
Safety is the primary issue at this point. The woman may want to
talk about the future of the relationship but workers will encourage
her to defer longer-term decisions and focus on immediate concerns, like what she is going to do *tonight?* Would she like to go to
a refuge? How can she ensure her safety? Crisis work deals with the
immediate crisis and considers further steps only after the matter
of safety has been dealt with.

It may be discovered at this point that the woman has been
threatened and that she is terrified of the consequences of taking
action. Violent men very often threaten to kill their partners,
especially if they are saying they will leave the marriage, or if the
man suspects she is going to expose the violence. Firearms are very
often involved and the police will be interested to get information
from her about what weapons there are in the house. A woman
may have had a gun held at her head and told she will be killed if
she tries to leave. Or the man may have fired a shot through the
floorboards and warned her that the next bullet will be through her
head.

WORK WITH THE SURVIVORS

DVCS workers aim to empower the woman, to help her take charge
of her own life. Friends and relatives may have underplayed the
significance of the violence and advised her to accept her lot, and

to try harder to make the relationship work. Crisis workers, on the other hand, treat her safety as the paramount issue. This is possibly the first time that the subject of safety has been discussed with her and the first time she has received acknowledgement that her life is in danger. Thus the intervention challenges her belief that she just has to put up with a life of violence. Many women are socialised to accept a subservient role in a relationship, to accept responsibility for its success or failure, and to accept whatever their male partner offers. Very often, the victims of violence have internalised the condemnation continuously imposed by their partner and believe that they are to blame, that it really is their fault for not having the dinner on the table when he got home at 2 am. Thus, the idea of valuing her own life, in preference to valuing her relationship, is a new one. So is the idea that she is a worthwhile person and not the pathetic failure portrayed by her husband. These challenges to her thinking may enable her to begin to disobey the patriarchal instructions which keep women living with their violent partners. It is difficult, however, to counter a process which has been occurring over a lifetime, and many women stay, hoping the violence will go away. Many are frightened of retaliation. Many stay because of their children—because they do not want their children to have to leave friends and school, or because they do not want to bring them up in poverty.

Support at the time of a crisis is vital. But not all support is empowering. Support given from the position of an expert who knows what is best for the woman simply confirms her belief that she is inadequate and unable to take charge of her life. In contrast, crisis workers offer victims of violence support based on the political belief that they are *survivors,* that is, that they have survived to this point despite the abuse, and that their lives are statements of resourcefulness, rather than weakness or failure. This respectful approach challenges the victim's low self-esteem and the lack of self-confidence generated by years of abuse.

The DVCS intervention is also aimed at giving the victim of violence accurate information about her options. It is most likely to be the case that she is unfamiliar with the legislation or the legal protection available. Workers know that all of the information given at this time of crisis may not be retained accurately and steps are taken to repeat the information until it is really assimilated. It is profoundly empowering to a woman to realise that the law is on her side and that it clearly states that she does not deserve violence. Even if she decides not to take any action, she at least has a clearer idea about what she can do to keep herself safe, about services available and about support she can receive. *She* must be the person who makes the decisions about her own life. This is the crux of the ideology of empowerment. Moreover, even if no immediate action is taken, it is very uplifting to a victim of violence to begin to believe that the violence is not her fault, and this new idea, in itself, has the potential to bring about long-term change in her life.

Once the victim has decided which option she wishes to exercise, crisis workers are able to facilitate practical action. This will depend in part on whether the police decide to arrest the offender. The action might be to remove the woman to a safe place, such as a refuge, or to accompany her the next day through the process of applying for an interim protection order at the Magistrates Court (see below).

However, it may be the case that the police and crisis workers leave the house without having been able to take any practical action, knowing that there is a strong possibility of further violence and that they will probably be called back to this address on a future occasion. Queensland figures suggest that for at least 50 per cent of 'domestics' attended by police, the police have been there before (Queensland Task Force, 1988: 407).

An independent evaluation of the work of the DVCS demonstrates that the DVCS has indeed been successful in its aim of empowering women. Here are some of the comments made by women interviewed in the evaluation. The question was: What has happened in your life since (the crisis intervention)?

> I have got a lot more peace of mind and rely on myself more and do not feel so bad about myself; I know that it is not all my fault.

> I am more sure of my self-worth. I enjoy family life with my children more. I joined CYSS and took on several courses which gave me self-respect and I have made many new friends. As a whole I am a new person.

> I feel free to be me. I don't feel trapped any more and it's the most wonderful feeling for me not to have to do things that I felt I had to do in my marriage, e.g. be forced into having sex if I didn't do as I was told. It's great not having to live with that any more.

A postscript on one questionnaire stated:

> The DVCS was a lifeline that I didn't know existed at that time. When speaking with me they were very careful to explain fully the options to me without trying to influence my decision in any way. Once I'd made my decision they were willing to assist with valuable information and support. I feel that, had I not sought their help, I would still be in a 'muddle' or even perhaps in a dangerous domestic situation. I cannot thank them enough for their presence.

Another questionnaire had the following note of thanks to the workers:

I wish you were around for my mother when she was younger. She just had to put up with the violence because that's all she knew and there was no-one like you around.

In all the cases above, the women had separated from their husbands. In the experience of the DVCS, one of the results of empowering a woman may well be that she decides to terminate a relationship with a violent man. Prior to the existence of the DVCS, the main aim of the police was to quieten the situation down and to encourage a reconciliation at almost any cost. The presence of the DVCS workers on the scene has thus dramatically altered the way 'domestics' are handled and had a substantial impact on outcomes.

CRISIS INTERVENTION AND PERPETRATORS

Most perpetrators of violence do not think there is anything wrong with what they have done. They are acting out of a belief in their right to own their female partner, and to do with this property whatever they think is justifiable, according to their own rules and standards and in some circumstances, their whim. An intervention by the police and DVCS workers challenges this whole way of thinking. It is a public statement that violence is not acceptable and is, in fact, against the law. As well as this, the DVCS workers' behaviour in supporting the victim, and their indifference to explanations, excuses and justification, further enhances the impression that this behaviour is not acceptable. Crisis interventions are thus bitterly resented by perpetrators.

DVCS workers will always have as their primary concern the safety of the victim. This will be an unusual experience for the perpetrator because, as 'man of the house', he will be used to being accorded superior status and preferential treatment from outsiders. The DVCS workers will spend time with him only after the woman's safety has been achieved and will outline the provisions of the laws relating to violent assault in the home and present the options he has.

Perpetrators will normally demand a fair hearing for their 'side of the story'. This is a revealing demand for the mere idea that there is another side of the story indicates a belief there can be a justification for violence. Justification usually involves blaming the woman for doing something he considers unacceptable, like not being awake when he gets home, not providing him with an acceptable meal, denying him sex, trying to stop him from having another bottle of beer, or not keeping the children quiet when he was watching television. His belief is that he is justified in using violence as a means of punishing her for these transgressions, and it is his ascribed superior status, because he is the man, which authorises him to punish.

Sometimes, rather than attempting to justify violence in this way a perpetrator may excuse himself by blaming external factors such as work stress, or an argument with a bloke at the pub. A man will sometimes come home and beat up his partner as if it were his right to use her as a punching bag. This is not about punishment, but is rather a consequence of his belief that the woman is his property and therefore meant to serve his every need.

The ownership-of-property attitude is most noticeable in situations where the woman has dared to have a mind of her own or a life of her own, in the form of a job or friends. Part of the patriarchal ideal is that women ought to be subordinate and inferior, so any demonstrated independence on the part of the woman, like wanting a job, or having a friend, or getting an education, threatens the man's superior status. He may then resort to physical violence, the one way he can prove his superiority, to retain his position of dominance and control.

The presence of crisis workers may enrage the perpetrator. Crisis workers will occasionally be sworn at, threatened, or verbally abused. Sometimes all of the police effort has to go into preventing further violence, and it may not be safe for the crisis workers to be there, even though the woman wants their presence.

While the victim of violence is usually receptive to the new ideas presented at the time of the intervention, it is not often a good time to present new and challenging ideas to the perpetrator. This is because his time of crisis has not yet happened. That time will come when he realises that he has lost his female partner, and sometimes his children, or when he finds himself removed from his own home by a domestic violence order. The intervention by police and DVCS workers is a time for justification and excuses and, even if the perpetrator is no longer being violent or aggressive, it is unlikely that he will hear the news being presented to him. In fact, very few perpetrators of violence ever reach the stage of acknowledging that their violence is unjustifiable and criminal. Very few perpetrators of violence ever adopt attitudes of equal regard for women and, even if they lose their partner, many move on to other relationships and behave in the same way.

DOMESTIC VIOLENCE ORDERS

The most effective way to prevent further violence immediately following a crisis intervention is for the police to arrest the perpetrator on an assault charge and to remand him without bail. This is almost never done. However, the Domestic Violence Ordinance enacted in the ACT in 1986 provides victims of violence with an alternative legal remedy—domestic violence protection orders, and more importantly, interim protection orders. Of course the existence of such a remedy does not automatically ensure its use, but the advice and support provided by DVCS workers have meant that large numbers of victims of violence have been able to avail themselves of the protection afforded by such orders. In fact, about 50 per cent of crisis interventions result in an application for an interim protection order, which is almost invariably granted. In 1990, 557 interim orders were granted in the ACT.

Following an episode of violence, and having been made aware of this possible remedy by the crisis workers, a woman may decide to go to court to seek such an order. Crisis workers go with her and support her in court and it is clear that without this support, many of the women concerned would be too fearful or intimidated to seek the legal protection available to them. From the point of view of the victim of violence, the DVCS plays a vital role in helping her obtain legal protection. From the point of view of the DVCS, domestic violence protection orders are a device which can be used to empower the victims of violence.

The process of obtaining a protection order may sometimes take many days and the perpetrator has the right to oppose the granting of the order. It cannot be relied upon, therefore, for immediate protection. To overcome this problem the legislation also made provision for *interim* protection orders and these are frequently used in emergency situations. An interim protection order can be obtained from the court the day after the violence, or on the Monday if the episode occurred during the weekend, and it can be obtained in the absence of the perpetrator. All that a woman need do to obtain an interim order is to make a sworn statement that she has been abused and is in fear of further violence. The order is served on the perpetrator as soon as possible by the police and comes into effect as soon as it is served. In determining an application for a protection order the court is required by the legislation to take account of the woman's need to be protected from violence or even harassment. Thus the legislation makes a clear statement that violence in the home is not acceptable.

Women usually make applications for interim protection orders without telling their male partners of their intention to do so. This gives them an opportunity to go to the court in safety and minimises the threat to their lives. Obviously, perpetrators of violence do not welcome the idea of their partner going to court to take out an order in an effort to stop the violence. Thus, women feel safer taking this step secretly. They are asked by the court staff to provide information to the police about his likely whereabouts, to assist police in serving the order. Sometimes, however, the offender is expecting the step to be taken and he successfully goes underground, making it difficult for the police to find him.

Interim protection orders can impose substantial restrictions on the behaviour of perpetrators. A particularly important aspect of this legislation is that orders may include a clause excluding the man from living at the same address as his spouse. More than half the interim orders granted by the court involve the eviction of men. Men may, in addition, be prohibited from being on premises where the spouse works or other premises specified by the court.

An order may also prohibit a man in general terms 'from contacting, harassing, threatening or intimidating the spouse'. This would cover such behaviour as telephone threats, leaving letters in the letterbox, writing messages in the frost on the windscreen of the car, knocking on the bedroom window during the night and so on, all of which are typical forms of harassment engaged in by men excluded from their homes. Furthermore, orders usually prevent the perpetrator from asking someone else, say a mutual friend or relative, to make contact for him.

A perpetrator may be prohibited from approaching within a specified distance of his spouse. This means that if a woman is in a public place, like a shopping centre or a pub, he may not approach her. If he is at the public place first, then the woman must leave.

The use of interim protection orders to exclude men from their homes has proved particularly controversial. There are competing values at stake here. On one hand, the spirit of the legislation is that women are entitled to be safe in their own homes. On the other is the idea that a man's home is his castle and that he has a right to reside there without interference by the law. Originally, some magistrates were reluctant to use the exclusion provision. As one said: 'I cannot remove a man from his own house.' Others took the view that if someone had to leave the house to bring the violence to an end, it should be the perpetrator, not the victim. Over time, and with the pressure of precedent, most magistrates are now prepared to give preference to the interests of victims in this respect, and it is now the case that most women who apply to have a man removed from the house are successful in their applications.

To our knowledge, the exclusion of men from their homes is almost unheard of in other states, even though the possibility exists in the relevant legislation. The difference is no doubt due in part to the progressive attitude of some of the personnel of the

ACT court. But it is also in part due to the activity of the DVCS in Canberra, encouraging victims of violence to make the fullest possible use of the very progressive legislation now in place. Most female victims of violence share the general presumption that a man has a right to remain in his own house and feel uneasy about seeking his exclusion. Crisis workers have pointed out to these women that they have as much right to the house as he and that in fact it is perfectly reasonable that he be required to leave the house rather than she, because he is the one committing the offence. It is clear that without the input from crisis workers fewer women would seek the removal of the perpetrator. This has been one of the more dramatic effects of the work of the DVCS.

The interim protection order normally remains in force until the so-called 'return' hearing, which must be within ten days of the initial hearing. The perpetrator may contest the order at this stage and evidence from both parties is then considered. The court decides whether or not the interim order will remain in place as a protection order for a period of twelve months. If the perpetrator does not attend the court on the date set down for the return hearing the protection order may be put in place 'by consent' and remains in place for twelve months.

An order is binding on both parties and neither may change its terms informally. If the woman decides that she wants to go to counselling with the offender, or to allow him to come to the house to collect the children for access, or wants to make phone contact asking for financial assistance, then a formal application for a variation must be made to the court. If there is a decision to reconcile then there must be a formal application to revoke the order. The outcome of these applications is determined by the court.

If an order is breached by a perpetrator he is guilty of an offence, punishable, in theory, by a fine not exceeding $1000 or imprisonment for up to six months. In practice, unfortunately, unless they involve further actual violence, most breaches go unpunished, especially if there are no witnesses, because they are regarded as 'technical breaches' only and thus undeserving of punishment. Nevertheless, many perpetrators are sufficiently intimidated by having a formal order served on them that they comply with its terms.

VIOLENCE NOT INITIALLY COVERED BY PROTECTION ORDERS

Some types of violence to which the DVCS has been called were not covered by the original legislation. The service has come across cases of teenage or adult sons beating their mothers, as well as a few cases of sibling violence and homosexual violence. Protection orders were not available under the original legislation in such cases. Accordingly, the DVCS was active on a review committee set up to consider the operation of the legislation, recommending that it be broadened to cover all household relationships. Legislation to this effect came into force in September 1990. Thus, the DVCS, set up as a result of a law reform commission recommendation, has itself contributed to further legislative change.

One area of particular concern to the DVCS which the legislation has now been extended to cover is violence by parents against children. Children occasionally ring the service, sometimes after seeing an advertisement or, alternatively, after a school talk by a crisis worker. These children are being routinely beaten by their fathers or mothers and sometimes sexually assaulted by them and it requires great courage on their part to ring, as they know that, if found out, they will suffer further beatings.

A typical story is that of a thirteen-year-old boy who called the DVCS one day. He had seen a television advertisement for the service on several occasions and had finally plucked up courage to ring. He had to miss school to do so, in order to be able to call without the knowledge of his parents. He had been beaten severely the night before by his father and promised a further beating the next day. He described how his mother colluded in the abuse and how, each time he tried to talk to her, asking for help to stop the violence, she told his father and he got another beating. He was overjoyed to hear about the possibility of escaping to a refuge and asked to be helped to do so. The law allows the DVCS to remove a child who asks to be taken to a safe place. Accordingly, the DVCS made an arrangement to place him in a youth refuge and to make a notification of child abuse to the youth advocate.

DVCS workers agreed to pick him up from the corner of his street at a time when his father was not home. When they arrived they discovered that the father had just returned unexpectedly and the boy could not get away. They were forced to withdraw, empty handed and fearful for the safety of the child. The boy was not allowed out of the house after returning home from school, had no access to any money, and had said he did not want to tell anyone at school what was happening at home. One option open to the DVCS in this situation was to call the police and to make a direct intervention. However, although under the amended legislation children are now able to apply for protection orders, assisted by the DVCS, at the time legal protection for the child was difficult to obtain. Thus, any intervention involving a confrontation with the father could easily have made matters worse for the boy. Accordingly, after much agonising, the DVCS decided not to intervene further. Such difficult and harrowing decisions are part of the daily work of the DVCS.

MALE VICTIMS

The question of male victims of violence is often raised by those opposed to the feminist philosophy of the DVCS. The fact is that less than 1 per cent of crisis interventions involve a man claiming to be a victim of a woman. These men are responded to in the same way as females and are given the same advice about protection orders and other options.

However, the circumstances of male victims are very different from those of women. First, in situations of female violence, DVCS workers very often discover that the woman has been a victim of violence for many years and she reaches a point where she has had enough and decides to retaliate. Sometimes it is the case that she has discovered that he is sexually abusing her children. It is often the case that she will use a weapon, and it may be in a situation where the man, having been excluded from the house by a domestic violence protection order being granted after years of violence from him, gains entry to her house by smashing a window. In these situations, her use of violence is in self-defence.

The second point is that these male 'victims' are rarely living in fear of their partner. Even when a man is not violent himself, nor abusive in any way, if a woman becomes physically abusive to him, if she punches or kicks him, he will normally be able to restrain her or to get away from her and leave the house. He is seldom actually injured by her violence. He is not fearful because he knows he has physical supremacy. It is difficult for a woman to injure a man unless she uses a weapon.

TELEPHONE WORK

Apart from direct crisis intervention, telephone work is another important aspect of DVCS activity. The secrecy and shame which surround domestic violence make it very difficult for many people to speak out about what is happening to them. Many women are too afraid to involve the police, and many want to protect their male partners from exposure. It is not unusual for the DVCS to be contacted anonymously by a woman who assumes workers would be shocked to know who her husband is. He may be a man of high standing in the community or even the church, or a member of the legal or medical professions. The woman will often assume that it is unusual for high-status men to be violent and this will reinforce her belief that she is in some way responsible.

The DVCS provides support, information and referral over the telephone, any time of the day or night. This means that people may speak about the violence anonymously. After two years of operation the monthly rate of calls was about 500, and about 65 per cent of these were first contacts. About 99 per cent of calls are from women.

Some victims of violence ring the day after the last violent episode, some ring a few days later, some ring at the time of the crisis and have to hang up before they have given their address. Because of the danger involved, the DVCS has a policy of not attending homes without the police, and if a caller is in immediate danger her permission is sought to call the police. Once permission is given, DVCS workers ask for police assistance and attend at the same time. If the address has not been given, nothing can be done. Most callers want to know what their options are. Some women call several times before they are ready to take action; some ring after years of violence, having finally had enough.

It is crucial in telephone work, as in direct crisis intervention, that crisis workers use an empowering approach and act out of a belief in a woman's own resources, even if the woman is unaware of those resources. At a time of crisis it is very easy to disempower a woman by taking over and making decisions for her. The intervention then begins to resemble the dynamic between her and her violent partner. It is most likely that before ringing DVCS, the victim of violence will have reached out to others, perhaps a friend, a mother or a counsellor, and will have been inadvertently disempowered, by having the violence belittled, or by being told that she should put up with it for the sake of marriage and family, or again, by having been told that 'it takes two to tango' and that the victim is at least partly responsible for the violence being perpetrated against her. It is dramatically different for a woman to be met with an empowering response, a response that comes from a belief in her right to be safe, and her right to equality, a response which in no way implicates her in the violence.

Another aspect of telephone work is to advise callers ringing on behalf of another person. Friends, relatives or neighbours often phone with concern about how best to respond to someone they know who is being abused, or a concern simply about the noise next door. This work involves training the caller in appropriate responses; that is, responses that do not blame the victim and which encourage the person to call themselves. Taking over the problem is not encouraged and it is explained to these callers that it is not empowering to a victim of violence to be given advice about what she should or should not do, nor is it empowering to have everything done for her. Callers are also encouraged to respond to crime as a crime and to phone the police at the time the violence is occurring.

PREVENTIVE EDUCATIONAL WORK

Apart from its crisis intervention and telephone work, the DVCS does a great deal of educational work in the community, not only to make people aware of the existence of the service but also to challenge existing societal attitudes and to inculcate the view that violence in the home is a crime and ought to be responded to as such. We shall mention just a few of these activities.

One major area of DVCS educational work is in high schools. It is symptomatic of the problem that the DVCS has sometimes had difficulty gaining permission to take its message into the classroom. Some teachers feel that children should not be told of the problem of violence in the home if they are not personally experiencing it.

The programmes the DVCS runs in high schools are aimed at empowering children through giving them a viable analysis of violence. They are helped to understand that perpetrators of violence are responsible for their own behaviour and that nobody deserves violence. They are taught survival skills and given ideas about how best they can act if someone in the house is being beaten up. They are given information about community resources, laws and so on. The overall aim is to foster the idea that violence in the home is a matter of public concern, and not a private, shameful secret. Children and young people are encouraged to report the crime of violence in the home to the police.

In order to help children who are themselves experiencing violence each child is given a card with the DVCS phone number and they are encouraged to ring anonymously if they prefer and to ring from a safe, private place. The programme aims to avoid personal disclosure in the classroom. However, in any class there will be children, with eyes averted, who are clearly in need of support. The aim is to have these children feel that the DVCS is reaching out to them, letting them know that there is a group of people to whom they can speak, who will understand, who will not blame, who will believe what they say, and who will take the danger they are in seriously.

The DVCS also runs educational programmes—workshops—for adults. A particularly important example was a workshop for

Anglican clergy. A group of Anglican women had for some time been pushing to have the church address domestic violence, and a course for clergy and other church workers was finally agreed to by the bishop. The DVCS ran a major part of the workshop and presented a feminist analysis of domestic violence. Participants were forced to grapple with the fact that some of the men amongst them read the scripture in church on Sunday and beat their wives during the week. Institutionalised gender inequality is nowhere more graphically displayed than in the teachings of the Bible and participants were asked to examine these teachings in the light of the feminist critique. The message clearly got through, for the bishop, who was present at the workshop, subsequently raised the matter in an official address to the synod. Here is part of what he said:

> ... domestic violence [is] substantially a male problem and church members [do] not appear to have any better record than non-church members. It is also a problem for the Church in that we may unconsciously reinforce attitudes of male superiority and dominance ...
>
> Let us beware of suggesting, as is common, that [violence] may be the women's fault, or that a wife-basher's or child-basher's behaviour is in any way explicable or excusable ...
>
> Let us also beware of promoting the idea that we are always on the side of holding marriage together at any cost ... [Under new legislation] perpetrators of domestic violence can rightly be excluded from their own homes and, in my opinion, should be. A soft response to this problem is not appropriate. (*The Canberra Times* 23 September 1989)

The educational work of the DVCS has also included lobbying government agencies at every opportunity to accept a feminist analysis of domestic violence. For example, the DVCS addressed the National Committee on Violence and made a written submission, outlining the experience of the crisis service and putting forward a grassroots perspective. The DVCS was not alone in this and the report by the National Committee commented that 'domestic violence was the most common subject of submissions made to the Committee by organisations'. The report gave some attention to domestic violence, and went so far as to acknowledge that the victims of domestic violence are 'overwhelmingly female' (1990: 33). But it did not accept the feminist analysis put to it by the DVCS and others. It argued that much of the violence in Australian society originated in the home, but rather than identifying attitudes of male dominance as the root cause it blamed the 'family', especially mothers:

> Families constitute the training ground for aggression ... [T]o the extent that families fail to instil non-violent values in their children, those children will be more likely to develop a repertoire of violent

behaviour ... [Furthermore,] there are correlations between aggression in children and certain characteristics of their parents, notably *maternal rejection* and parental use of physical punishment and threat. (1990:xxiv, emphasis added)

This is not the place to analyse the committee's conclusion. The point we wish to make is simply that, despite the failure of the DVCS and other feminist groups to win acceptance for their viewpoint, the committee's acknowledgement of the problem of domestic violence is evidence of the impact of this lobbying activity.

The DVCS is being watched by other crisis services around Australia and is regarded by many as providing the best model for effective crisis intervention. Interstate groups seek input from the DVCS from time to time. For example, the Tasmanian Crisis Service asked the DVCS for some specialised training, and a workshop for the staff of the three Tasmanian centres was arranged.

The DVCS is also regularly asked to provide in-service training for the staff of other agencies in Canberra which come in contact with domestic violence—hospitals, the ambulance service, emergency housing, welfare, legal aid and so on. This work is not only about achieving practical cooperation, but is also an opportunity to educate, to raise awareness of the issues involved in violence in the home and to politicise the subject. Many of the members of the helping professions are particularly imbued with the idea that they should not make value judgements in working with clients and that they should adopt a 'fair and balanced' approach in dealing with domestic violence. The DVCS encourages these people to make the judgement that violence is wrong, indeed, criminal, and to react to their clients accordingly.

CONCLUSION

The primary role of the DVCS is to help women who are victims of violence to make decisions which will put an end to the violence they experience. This is not just a band-aid function. It is based on a feminist analysis of violence and is designed to help women take charge of their own lives. The DVCS also takes every opportunity to expose social attitudes which condone violence by men against women in their homes and to promote the view that such violence is criminal and ought to be responded to as such. Thus, the service is not just an agency for helping individuals. It is also a source of social change, seeking an end to the system of gender inequality out of which domestic violence arises.

7 The police and the crisis service

An effective response to domestic violence depends on close collaboration between the police and the DVCS: the job of the police is to stop the violence and perhaps arrest the perpetrator, while that of the crisis workers is to help the victim to take steps to protect herself. In theory, this is a productive division of labour. However, it is fraught with complexity; a more unlikely liaison than that between feminist women and male police is hard to imagine. The surprise was not that working relations with the police turned out to be difficult, but that they were not more so.

The police force is a hierarchical, male-dominated institution, built on the assumption of the right to use force to uphold the law. This creates something of an ideological dilemma for the DVCS. To work effectively with the police force it must accept its hierarchical form and the fact that individuals within such an organisation exercise legitimate power over each other by virtue of their position in the hierarchy. At the same time the DVCS holds that male assault in the home is an exercise of power by men over women, an analysis which generalises into a critique of all relationships which involve the exercise of power by one individual over another.

The working relationship between the DVCS and the police is complicated by the fact that some male police, like many others in our society, tend to have a very negative view of feminists and subscribe to the popular stereotype of a feminist as a woman who lacks intelligence, wears overalls and hates men. A further problem for some police is that feminists claim that *women* are the victims of spouse assault—they are therefore sexist. Given this attitude, some difficulties were to be expected.

THE POLICE AND 'DOMESTICS'

In spite of these difficulties, the police do have a vested interest in making the relationship work, for domestic disputes have always been one of their major problems. The Queensland Task Force on domestic violence estimated that about 20 per cent of calls to police concern domestic disputes (1988: 119), while in the ACT the corresponding figure is 30 per cent (AFP, n.d.: 125) In the western suburbs of Sydney, up to 35 per cent of calls, that is, more than one in three, are from women who have been bashed by the men they live with (Hatty, 1988: 100). As for the total time involved, the New South Wales Police Force 'identified domestic violence as being second only to traffic incidents in terms of police workload' (Mugford, 1989: 4), while Scutt (1982: 117) suggests that on some calculations more than half of police working time is taken up with domestic violence. Whatever the figures, it is clear that domestic violence is a major aspect of police work. It is, therefore, very much in police interests that the relationship with the DVCS works effectively, for in the long run the activity of the DVCS may be expected to reduce the police workload.

Traditionally, like the rest of society, police have not regarded violence in the home as a crime, but as a 'problem'. Police policy in responding to violence in the home has been to adopt a conciliatory, peace-making role, and it has been an unpalatable aspect of police work for officers to have to play social worker or counsellor. But that is what was asked of them. Arrest was used only as a last resort. Moreover, even when they wanted to make arrests, they felt hampered by inadequate police powers. All of this has meant that in the past the police response to domestic violence has been somewhat inadequate.

Senior police have recognised this inadequacy and recognised, too, that the new legislation, coupled with the establishment of the DVCS, demands changes in police attitudes and policies. As expressed in the police handbook on domestic violence (AFP, n.d.: 1):

> The police role in the handling of 'domestic violence' situations in the ACT has undergone a significant change with the introduction of new legislation. As with most legislation there are some positive gains and some aspects which will place a more onerous responsibility upon police.

SENIOR POLICE

In discussing relationships between the DVCS and the police it is convenient to distinguish three categories of police: senior police, middle level, supervisory police and patrol police. These distinctions need to be kept in mind in what follows.

An attitude of goodwill on the part of senior police towards the DVCS was evident even before the establishment of the service. Senior police were committed to the concept of a crisis service and a police liaison officer (Chief Inspector Euan Walker) was a member of the various committees involved in the setting up of the service. Here he was confronted by dedicated feminist women who upheld their ideology with tenacity but also with a sensitivity to the difficulty it posed for the police. The police were, at first, very skeptical of a group which insisted that women are the overwhelming victims of domestic violence and which wanted to include a commitment to work towards the empowerment of women and children in its constitution. As we saw in an earlier chapter, the Australian Federal Police (AFP) protested about this inclusion. They were unhappy with the notion that violence in the home was an outcome of gender inequality. However, the police commitment to the service was such that they maintained their membership of the various management committees. This commitment was vital to the very existence of the DVCS. The police could survive happily without a DVCS, but the service would have failed totally in the absence of police cooperation.

The DVCS was greatly impressed by the goodwill shown by senior police during the drafting of guidelines specifying just how the collaboration would work in practice. They were quite prepared to remove some guidelines which offended members of the DVCS management committee, and to negotiate and reword others. A striking example concerned the following clause orginally drafted by the police: 'The DVCS staff will acknowledge their secondary role and will abide by police directions ... ' While committee members accepted that police would remain in ultimate control at the scene of a crisis intervention, the reference to 'secondary role' was felt to demean the DVCS workers unnecessarily. The police, accordingly, agreed to its removal. It is a tribute to the people involved that, despite opposing views and politics, working guidelines were developed to the satisfaction of both groups and without either feeling too compromised.

The commitment of senior officers to the DVCS is obvious in the way that the AFP responds to complaints from the DVCS. Requests for meetings with the ACT's chief police officer, the assistant commissioner, have always been granted and there has always been a willingness to examine existing procedures and policies in order to respond to DVCS complaints. This flexibility and concern for the effective operation of the DVCS is illustrated by the following events.

Immediately after the establishment of the DVCS, it became clear that it was not being called to many 'domestics'. When this matter was first raised, a meeting was arranged between the DVCS coordinator and the assistant commissioner and procedures were changed immediately. Previously, crisis workers would be called to an address at the time of an invitation being extended by the women (the procedures regarding invitations have been explained in chapter 6). This meant that patrol police had to wait up to half an hour for them to arrive. But once peace and quiet had been established they were often too busy to wait for DVCS workers to arrive. So this early arrangement turned out not to be conducive to receiving invitations. A suggestion was made that the police operations centre call the DVCS immediately they had a patrol car on the way, and that DVCS workers wait in the vicinity until receiving an invitation, which would be relaid to them, either in person by the patrol police, or on the car phone from police operations, once they had been advised by the patrol police. The assistant commissioner bypassed normal bureaucratic procedures and had this suggestion implemented immediately.

One other example of the way in which good relations between senior police and the DVCS have facilitated an effective response to domestic violence is worth mentioning. Women sometimes call the police complaining that a man who has been excluded from the house by a protection order is back, harassing her, in breach of the order. The patrol police who attend the call may regard the breach as 'technical' only, there having been no further violence, and decide not to arrest the man. On various occasions when this has happened, the DVCS has rung the station commander the next day and suggested that the breach ought to be taken seriously. The result has often been a police decision to summons the perpetrator for the breach.

MIDDLE-LEVEL POLICE: UNEARTHING THE CONFLICT

The commitment of senior police was really put to the test when the DVCS coordinator drew their attention to the disrespectful treatment of crisis workers by a minority of patrol police. Operational guidelines agreed to by the DVCS and the police require the police to 'treat the DVCS staff as they would any other professional field workers and service providing agencies within the ACT'. The guidelines also require that conflict not be addressed on the job, but referred to the DVCS coordinator and the police liaison officer for resolution.

The acting assistant commissioner was concerned about this disrespect shown by some of his officers and promised to do something about it. He organised a meeting of all supervisory police, about 45 in total, all males except for one, which was intended to give the DVCS a forum. The DVCS was represented by the coordinator and one crisis worker, who outlined the aims of the service and raised some of the difficulties workers were having on the job.

The meeting was a heated one with various police raising objections to the way crisis workers were doing the job. A few strongly resented what they saw as the interference of the DVCS in police activity. Critical remarks were also made about the sexism of the DVCS. Alarming attitudes were revealed that day by a few officers present, attitudes which differed from those of more senior police. Some thought that women bring violence on themselves: 'they stay at home while the man is out working and then cause trouble when he gets home, so they get what they deserve'. Others felt that women should know their place (meaning in the kitchen) and some believed that women must enjoy violence, otherwise they would leave. A 'blame the victim' mentality was evident in some of those present, a mentality which is widespread in the community as a whole. It is important to stress that these were not the attitudes of all of those present. Nor are they peculiar to Canberra police. A Sydney study has reported quite horrifying attitudes among some police in that city (Hatty, 1988).

The next move from senior police came during a difficult period for the AFP. Their assistant commissioner had been assassinated, they were facing the restructuring of their institution involving the removal of several layers in their hierarchy, and regionalisation was occurring. Morale was low. Yet senior officers, in particular Acting Assistant Commissioner Alan Mills, and the newly appointed Assistant Commissioner Brian Bates, still found time to consider relations with the DVCS.

They suggested that the station commanders for all three of the Canberra police regions be appointed DV liaison officers, and thus become points of contact for the DVCS coordinator. Previously only one senior officer had been in daily contact with the DVCS. This officer had the responsibility of checking computer listings each day to make sure that the DVCS had been involved in every call to a 'domestic'. Any follow-up work was also done through this officer. With regionalisation, there were to be three officers performing this role in relation to their own region. The assistant commissioner directed that there be weekly meetings between the three station commanders and the DVCS coordinator until relations improved and until such time as it was felt that the meetings could occur with less frequency. After a few months the meetings became monthly, with telephone contact happening on an almost daily basis.

It gradually became clear that the original meeting with supervisory police had not been a waste of time. Many of them seemed to have changed their attitudes to DVCS workers and over time had come to accept the legitimacy of the DVCS role.

POLICE ON THE JOB

While having senior police on side and sympathetic to the aims of the DVCS is a tremendous advantage, relations between crisis workers and police on the job, understandably, are sometimes problematic. One of the areas of greatest conflict between crisis workers and patrol police concerns the question of whether to arrest the perpetrator. It is very often clear that a criminal assault has occurred, and the new legislation makes it easier than it was formerly to obtain convictions. Some police, however, are reluctant to arrest perpetrators and view any suggestion from crisis workers that they should do so as interference.

There are several reasons why arrest is seldom the police response. First, there is the police ideology that 'there are two sides to every story'. A fairly typical scenario when the police arrive is for the man to take over and tell what he sees as *the* story of what happened. It is a common expectation that men will take the lead in these situations. The experience of the crisis workers is that this story will generally involve justification, excuses and gross understatement of his part in the incident. It is a rare man who will accurately describe the extent of his violence, especially to the police. In accordance with their training, police listen carefully to this story. Men often have an ability to be convincing, credible and seductively friendly in these situations, and it may happen that a certain camaraderie develops between the man and the police. According to police they sometimes even foster this camaraderie in order to calm men down. As the man's story unfolds, the police may discover that his wife is having an affair, or that she has not been behaving as a wife should, and in their minds this will explain the violence and even, to some extent, excuse it. Indeed, this information may lead some police to hold her at least partly responsible for the violence of which she has been a victim.

A second reason for police reluctance to arrest is a tendency to minimise the seriousness of the offence. Police will generally, although not always, take the matter seriously if there is clear evidence of injury, but if there is no blood or bruising on exposed parts of the body, they will sometimes play down what has happened with comments like 'They have just had a bit of a tiff'; or 'She hasn't copped much of a beating'; or 'She's very upset but she will settle down'.

A third factor is the police experience of taking cases to court and feeling that they are wasting the court's time. There is a view among some magistrates that, with the advent of the new legislation, the appropriate response to much domestic violence is for a women to take out a protection order, rather than for the police to arrest the man on an assault charge. The view is that arrest is unnecessarily punitive, and in any case, results in unnecessarily complex court processes. Moreover, some magistrates see it as their responsibility to uphold the values of marriage and family and believe that orders allow for the possibility of reconciliation, while arrest makes this less likely. Along with the rest of society, they do not always see assault by a man against his wife in the same light as assault on a stranger. Understandably, when magistrates give expression to such views from the bench, the police feel that they have been made to appear foolish.

Fourth, there is a great deal of effort involved for a police officer in taking a matter to court. Statements must be taken which are generally handwritten or typed and this process is tedious and time consuming. The officer must consider seriously whether the occurrence of an offence can be proved, not just whether it has occurred, and whether there is sufficient evidence to counteract the anticipated denial of the offence on the part of the defendant. This is typically a problem with domestic violence because in nearly all cases there are no witnesses other than the two parties involved.

Fifth, many police quote experiences where a woman has wanted a man arrested and then changed her mind the next day. They also fear that if the matter does get to court the woman may 'let them down' at the last minute by refusing to give evidence. Under the new legislation women are compellable witnesses; that is, they can be made to give evidence, even when they do not want their husband charged with an offence. In practice, however, if a woman chooses not to cooperate there is not much that can be done to salvage a prosecution.

Finally, some police are reluctant to arrest a man if they consider that the relationship has a chance of surviving, and they are very concerned not to be seen as breaking up families and marriages. On some occasions, these concerns about marriages and families staying intact override concerns about safety of the members.

PATROL POLICE ATTITUDES TO THE DVCS

One year after it began operation, the DVCS had itself externally evaluated by a consultant on contract. As part of this evaluation, a sample of police was interviewed and the results proved very demoralising for the DVCS. Apart from positive comments by the station commanders, the comments from police on the job were mostly negative and showed an alarming misunderstanding of the function of the DVCS. In the main, police believed that the role of the DVCS is or ought to be a conciliatory, peace-making one, aimed at restoring marriages and families to harmony. They were consistently critical of the DVCS for not aiming to reconcile the parties, and for not listening attentively to both sides of the story. This had been their role before the advent of the service and they assumed that this should be the role of the DVCS, despite the spirit of the new legislation.

Furthermore, they were highly critical of 'sexism' displayed by the DVCS in assuming that the woman was always the victim and for ignoring the fact that she may have provoked the attack. Some patrol police felt that this problem might be remedied by the employment of male crisis workers and made recommendations to this effect. It is worth noting, in response to this point, that the DVCS does not have a formal policy restricting employment to women. However, an all-female staff would seem to be appropriate, since the victims of domestic violence, almost all women, feel more at ease with female workers, having just been beaten up by a man.

Police surveyed in the evaluation also expressed resentment at being told by crisis workers 'how to do their job'; for example, they resented any suggestion that the perpetrator should be arrested. Finally, crisis workers were criticised for dressing too casually, for not being experienced enough, and for not having formal qualifications.

These last three criticisms require some response. In relation to dress, crisis workers deliberately dress neutrally in order to minimise the social distance between themselves and the women they are seeking to help. As for the police concern about qualifications, although we do not believe the matter to be of great significance, it should be noted that a large number of crisis workers have tertiary degrees. More importantly, given their background in refuge work, most crisis workers have far more experience in the area of domestic violence than any other group of workers.

It is worth quoting a few of the police responses to give some direct evidence of their views. According to one:

> They [the crisis workers] take the side of the female always and at one domestic they even told us to arrest a male. The female wished not to complain. We were told by the male to leave the premises so we did. They still wondered why we didn't do anything.

This comment demonstrates vividly several of the points we have been making: first the concern about bias, secondly the resentment at being told how to do their job, third an unwillingness to make an arrest without the cooperation of the victim. Another policeman had this to say:

The main weakness [of the DVCS] seems to be their siding on the female's side all the time. I don't particularly like them telling me how to do my job. Also they never seem to listen to the male point of view. If a male was flogged by his wife, which has happened on numerous occasions, they still take the side of the female and offer her solutions instead of him. Once a D.V. order is served there should be a period in which reconciliation between the parties can be considered, instead of cutting them off from each other altogether.

Despite the mainly negative tone of the evaluations, there were some positive comments about the usefulness of the crisis workers, the importance of the DVCS role and the appropriateness of the workers not being in a uniform. Reference was also made to the fact that some people feel easier about talking to crisis workers rather than police, the appropriateness of victims of violence having women to talk to, the impressive knowledge of crisis workers of the legislation and services available to victims, their ability to provide on-the-spot support and practical assistance and the reduction in workload which the DVCS has meant for police. Here is one such comment:

In most cases, the DVCS has been helpful to the police. In some cases, the DVCS has taken the women and children away from a very hostile environment and provided accommodation as well as transport. This service has been of great help.

It hardly needs to be said that the views expressed by police in the survey are consistent with the experience of the crisis workers on the job. They encounter some police who are supportive of the DVCS and appreciative of the work it does, and others who are critical.

Station commanders were also interviewed in the survey and their only criticism was that DVCS workers were not familiar enough with the police role and their powers in relation to domestic violence matters. Apart from this one observation, they were appreciative of the role and functioning of the DVCS.

AN IMPROVING RELATIONSHIP

Given the extent, revealed in the survey, of the belief that the DVCS was a counselling service, the DVCS asked for a second meeting with middle-level supervisory police to correct the misunderstanding. At this meeting it was explained that counselling has proved largely ineffective in dealing with domestic violence and that, in any case, the mandate of the DVCS was not to counsel the parties with a view to reconciliation, but to intervene in crises in order to secure the safety of victims and to advise them on the options available for their protection. The supervisory police present agreed to hold meetings with their staff to correct the misunderstanding. What was really striking about this meeting was that its tone was quite different from that of the first. On this occasion, the audience was responsive and understanding. Clearly the day-to-day association of the two organisations was having an impact. The supervisory police reported that patrol police had increasing respect for DVCS workers and were increasingly appreciative of the work of the service. This difference in attitude at the meeting was evident to all. A senior officer commended DVCS for persevering after the initial meeting and commented that 'we have all come a long way'.

A suggestion coming out of this meeting was that the coordinator visit each station every two to three months to speak with patrol police and to be available to listen to their comments about crisis workers. This was agreed to and these meetings have proved useful in giving patrol police an opportunity to be heard and to feel that their complaints, as well as those of the crisis workers, are being recognised and taken seriously.

As for the criticisms of crisis workers made in the survey by station commanders, the DVCS asked the police to hold a training day for crisis workers to instruct them on the police role, police powers of arrest and the laws relating to domestic violence situations. This turned out to be a further exercise in building trust between the two organisations. The training was organised and facilitated by the police training academy and was excellent in its focus, timing, and respectful delivery.

In summary, given the divergent philosophies and organisational styles, the collaboration between the police and the DVCS was bound to be difficult. Misunderstandings and mistrust were evident on both sides from the outset. But effective crisis intervention depends on close collaboration between the two organisations. And this is what has happened. Despite the differences, the job gets done. The DVCS and the police have worked steadily to improve the relationship and over time it has indeed improved. This has been in no small measure due to the commitment of senior police to making it work. The way in which the DVCS and the police have been able to cooperate in the ACT is now being seen by some police forces interstate as a model which they might profitably follow.

8 The crisis service and the legal system

Many legal system personnel have a tendency to hold the victim in some way responsible for the violence perpetrated against her, as does most of society. In addition, they have great difficulty understanding why victims are such half-hearted and inadequate complainants and witnesses. This chapter discusses the difficulties which victims have in getting the legal system to take them seriously and to treat them sympathetically. It deals also with the setbacks and successes the DVCS has had in attempting to get the legal system to respond more adequately.

THE ROLE OF THE CRISIS SERVICE

The DVCS generally arranges appointments with the Legal Aid duty solicitor for women they have had contact with during the preceding night. If by chance Legal Aid has already represented the perpetrator on any matter, it is unable to represent the woman, as this would place it in a conflict of interest. In these circumstances the DVCS may assist with appointments with solicitors in private practice. After discussions with the solicitor, the applicant must go before a magistrate to get the order. Crisis workers accompany women throughout these lengthy processes, and in particular are present in the courtroom, where their support is especially crucial.

A court appearance is a daunting and fearful process, especially for women who are socialised to be in awe of men in high places. The world of the law is a formal, largely male world, where strict rules and rigorous procedures apply. Hearings are conducted in sometimes incomprehensible legal language. There are status symbols like black robes, high benches, and special entrances for magistrates, and rituals such as bowing on entering the court. The effect of all of these is to engender awe in those who must face the court. Crisis workers are able to support a woman just by being with her so that she does not feel completely alone in this strange and alienating place. They are able to empower her by explaining what is happening, and by encouraging her to feel more confident about what she is doing. Because of their experience in dealing with these situations, they can to some extent demystify and normalise the process for her.

Crisis workers cannot normally appear as witnesses. They know the woman's story in detail, having seen the injuries and dealt with the woman's terror and despair, but typically they have not seen the violence in question and so cannot testify on her behalf. Neither do they legally represent the woman in court. Thus, when she is actually giving evidence, they are not in a position to prompt her, to remind her to tell the story about the knife, or to recount the incident of the broken ribs. Many women, quite irrationally, feel great shame about their injuries and need to be encouraged to reveal them. The court does not understand this. The crisis workers do. It is thus extremely frustrating when they are unable to ensure that the woman makes the best possible case for herself. Court procedures effectively muzzle the crisis workers at critical moments.

One way in which the DVCS has managed to have a formal input into court proceedings is to have its personnel called as expert witnesses at sentencing hearings. At such times they have been able to explain to the magistrate the likely effect of various sentences on the woman. If, for example, as has often happened in these cases, the man has threatened to kill his wife if she gives evidence against him in an assault case, and if the magistrate declines to imprison the offender, his wife may have to go into hiding immediately following his conviction. The DVCS may then be involved in helping her to relocate, perhaps to another state.

But statements on behalf of the victim at the time of sentencing have not been routine, and it is, in any case, a magistrate's decision as to whether he will allow such testimony. The DVCS has had meetings with the chief magistrate on various occasions to express disquiet about the effect on victims of some of the sentences imposed on perpetrators and he has proved appreciative of the DVCS input and anxious, too, that 'victim impact statements' become a formalised part of court proceedings. He has publicly advocated that the law be changed to facilitate such statements.

It should be said, in passing, that although the chief magistrate declined to have the court represented on the management committee of the DVCS, on the grounds that it was a feminist organisation and any formal association with the DVCS might compromise the gender neutrality of the court, in practice he has been very supportive of the DVCS, facilitating its work and encouraging close consultation.

THE PROBLEM OF VICTIM CREDIBILITY

One of the greatest problems facing victims of violence in court apearances is their lack of credibility in the eyes of the court. The issue is essentially one of gender inequality. Women get upset, indeed afraid, and do not present well in court. Men, on the other hand, are generally not so daunted by solicitors and courts and handle themselves in ways which are more appropriate in the eyes of the court. Many lawyers are unable to see beyond the appearances and are quite convinced that the pleasant, affable, even charming man before them could not possibly be capable of violence. Many of the court staff, most lawyers and all magistrates in Canberra are men and naturally understand men better than they do women. Men will judge women according to their own values and beliefs. For example, they will generally judge someone on how logical and in control the person is, for these are good male traits.

A man's rapport with court personnel is also enhanced by his dress. Our society seems to value appearance in a way which is quite bewildering. An offender who has beaten his wife, held her captive, threatened her with death, demeaned and humiliated her, can put on a suit, have a shave and comb his hair and is immediately assumed to be a decent man. As a court official observed of one offender, 'he scrubs up well'.

As for the woman, she is likely to be emotional, which tends to make formal lawyers uncomfortable; her body is probably hurting, but she cannot speak about it; she may feel dreadful guilt; and she often presents her story in an unconvincing way. She long ago gave up any positive ideas she may have had about her appearance because she has been told for years that she is ugly and stupid and why would he bash her anyway if she were not. It will probably not make sense to her that she should dress up to give a good impression. If a woman does dress up and makes an effort to give a good impression, she may still not be taken seriously. Observers may think to themselves: 'If the violence is that bad how could she be looking as good as she does?' Because it is all so hard, so frightening and strange, she will probably change her mind a lot, be quite confused about what she should do, and even forget vital pieces of information which would help her case. Being irrational, illogical and indecisive is sometimes held against her and this behaviour can seriously detract from her credibility in the eyes of the court.

Another way women lose credibility in the eyes of the legal profession is when they return to a violent man, after taking out an order, or calling the police, or leaving him. These women are criticised for their apparent lack of good sense, for their ambivalence about the relationship and for their weakness. If a woman goes back to a violent man, a judgement is inevitably made that the violence cannot be all that bad, or that she must have exaggerated it. Some lawyers, like many in the general population, even believe that if she goes back into the relationship it must be because she likes the violence.

These views reveal a complete lack of understanding of women's attempts to correct what is so terribly wrong in their lives. So often women return to their violent partners because of the way society values marriage and the family and because of their loyalty to these values. So often they want the relationship and the family, without the violence, and they are therefore very susceptible to the promises that violent men make that the violence will never happen again. They return out of desperation and out of hope that perhaps things could be different. They are beaten up again, of course, and they may or may not return to the legal system for help. If they do return it is often not help and understanding they receive, but disrespect and humiliation.

Take, for example, the case of one woman who took out an interim order and then revoked it at the return hearing a few days later. She gave no explanation. She was asked if he was making her revoke it. She said no. Of course he was. He had threatened more violence unless she revoked it and told her that he would kill her if she mentioned this threat in court. She left the court, returned to her flat, and was beaten up yet again by the man. The police had not in fact been able to serve the order on him in the preceding days as he had gone into hiding. Part of her reason for revoking the order was that she knew that the police had not been able to find him and that the order was therefore of no use. This was her third attempt to take out a protection order and the third revocation. Each time, the man suspected what was happening and managed to elude the police, thus preventing service of the order. However, the effect of her three applications and subsequent revocations, was to undermine her credibility in the eyes of the law.

Most people have a capacity to feel a certain level of compassion and empathy for the plight of others, based either on their own experience or on imagination. They can, for example, feel compassion for people hurt in car crashes or other accidents. But in the case of domestic violence society often shows little compassion for the victims. Rather, there is judgement, criticism and a lack of empathy. These attitudes are unfortunately all too apparent in the way victims of violence are sometimes treated by the law.

In summary, the legal system frequently shows little understanding of the predicament of a battered woman. She has been beaten up and terrorised by a man but is then expected to be warm, friendly and respectful to men. She is expected to know what she wants to do. She is expected to make sense, when nothing in her life makes any sense to her. But perhaps this insensitivity is to be expected, for no-one can really know how a beaten woman feels— except other beaten women.

PRIVATE LAWYERS

The crisis service has a good deal of contact with private solicitors, either as the legal representatives of perpetrators, or sometimes, representing the victims of violence. These lawyers are steeped in a legal ideology which in many ways works against the interests of domestic violence victims. In addition, there has been a sad lack of understanding of domestic violence among some of these members of the legal profession, especially a lack of understanding of the human tragedy involved, as well as the general prejudice against women described earlier. Finally, some private lawyers are critical of the role of the DVCS and its feminist philosophy. Cooperation is difficult to achieve under these circumstances. In what follows we shall examine the way in which certain elements of legal ideology and practice make cooperation difficult to achieve.

The courtroom process is a contest, a competition, conducted according to certain rules. In representing a client in court, the lawyer's role is not to pursue truth or substantive justice; it is to engage in a contest on behalf of the client. The lawyer's responsibility is to present the client in the best possible light and to challenge or seek to discredit any evidence against the client. That is the nature of the adversarial system. That is the lawyer's job.

The following may serve as an illustration of what this can mean in practice. A private solicitor was representing a male perpetrator who looked as though he might end up serving time in prison. A crisis worker was in court with the woman, supporting her through what turned out to be a harrowing process. The solicitor was worried about the psychological effect of this scene on the magistrate. The fact that the woman needed such support might well suggest just how upset she was and this might work against the interests of his client. Accordingly, he formally requested that the crisis worker be removed. The woman's lawyer objected on the grounds that the woman was entitled to such support, whereupon the solicitor suggested that if the crisis worker were allowed to stay, he should be entitled to bring in support for his client in the form of several of his male friends who were waiting outside. This argument was apparently effective, and the magistrate ruled that the crisis worker should leave.

It should be pointed out that on an earlier occasion another solicitor had attempted to have a crisis worker removed from a hearing over which the chief magistrate was presiding. On that occasion the request had been refused, the chief magistrate stating that the crisis workers had a legitimate and important role in court. The DVCS was delighted with this ruling.

A further feature of legal ideology which is significant in the present context is that, generally, the choice of whom a solicitor represents is not guided by moral or ethical principles, the only principle in this respect being that every person has the right to legal representation. Thus a lawyer who represents a victim of violence one day may represent a perpetrator of violence the next. It is part of the legal belief system that they should be prepared to do so. For crisis workers, and especially for female victims, this willingness to represent perpetrators provokes considerable suspicion. A woman who sees her lawyer side with a perpetrator of violence in another matter finds it hard to believe that when her turn comes this lawyer will really be on her side.

Related to this is the lawyer's role of taking instructions from the client and acting on those instructions. The problem is that if the client is unable to give instructions, the lawyer is unable to act. If the client cries a lot, for example, some lawyers may have great difficulty dealing with her. Their response in this situation may be to advise her not to cry in court because of 'the way it will look', an explicit acknowledgement of the bias which is likely to operate against her. Some of these lawyers have little understanding of the plight of their clients. Again, this is not surprising. The legal process does not require that lawyers have any particular sympathy with or understanding of their clients, merely that they represent their interests in a strictly legal sense in the courtroom. Indeed, like many other professionals, lawyers are often fearful of 'overinvolvement' with their clients.

In contrast, crisis workers are thoroughly involved. They are specialists in matters of violence in the home and have a long-term commitment to the interests of victims. Theirs is a far more active role than that of the solicitor. They are on the side of the victim of violence in a far more total way and their response to her inarticulateness is to prompt, encourage and empower her in various ways. They can see beyond her inadequacy as a complainant and witness in a way that many solicitors cannot.

Yet another element of legal ideology occasionally in evidence is a misplaced insistence by some lawyers on the criminal law principles that a person must be presumed innocent until proved guilty and that accused persons have the right to defend themselves in court. The new legislation enables women to obtain interim protection orders on their own evidence and without the perpetrator having been notified of the application. (He can, however, oppose it at the return hearing which must occur within ten days.) A number of private lawyers are highly critical of these so-called *ex parte* applications, that is, applications in which one party is not present, and see them as violating the fundamental rights of defendants.

The fact is, however, that an application for a domestic violence order is not a criminal matter and does not involve any finding of guilt on the part of the perpetrator. It imposes requirements on his future behaviour, any violation of which would indeed be a criminal matter. An application for a domestic violence order is a civil law matter in which no-one, formally speaking, is a defendant and no-one is at risk of being punished. Thus any appeal to the presumptions of the criminal law is misplaced.

We might note, in passing, that even in the criminal law the presumption that a defendant is innocent until proved guilty does not always apply. There are many circumstances where the need to ensure effective law enforcement has overridden the presumed right of defendants in this regard (Hopkins, 1981). To be more specific, there are many laws which specify that defendants are presumed *guilty* unless they can prove innocence. To give just one example, a person in possession of more than a specified quantity of marijuana is presumed to be in possession for the purposes of sale, rather than personal use (a less serious offence), unless he or she can prove otherwise.

Sometimes the objection is based not on criminal law principles but, more vaguely, on the 'civil liberties' of perpetrators. This argument simply ignores the right of a woman to live free from violence. The fact is that the *ex parte* process allows immediate legal protection for the victim, and was introduced because of the unsatisfactory delays which occurred when both parties had a right to be present. The legislature saw fit to give preference to women's rights in this very limited situation and this is something which some private solicitors simply cannot accept.

In the preceding discussion we have shown how the legal beliefs and occupational role of private solicitors are in conflict with the beliefs and occupational role of the DVCS. It is also the case that a minority of solicitors, by no means all, simply fail to accept that the DVCS has any role in matters they consider to be legal and therefore their own domain. We should stress that this is not true of all private solicitors—some of them are very appreciative of the work of the DVCS and good working relationships have developed in these circumstances.

The problem of conflicting occupational roles is most apparent at meetings between women and their solicitors, prior to a court hearing. As mentioned earlier, private solicitors are used when women are not eligible for legal aid. If a woman wishes, and she usually does, a crisis worker will go with her to this meeting.

Victims of violence are often intimidated by a male solicitor, formally attired, sitting in an imposing office behind his large desk, and they find themselves tongue-tied and unable to present their story effectively. The crisis worker therefore prompts the women, fills in details and makes suggestions as to how matters might proceed. Some solicitors feel that such an approach is 'interfering', 'coming between him and his client', 'looking over his shoulder', 'telling him how to do his job'.

Matters have sometimes come to a head with the solicitor refusing to continue to represent the woman unless the crisis worker leaves. The woman is then in a bewildering predicament. She is being asked to give up the support she has been relying upon since the crisis intervention, perhaps the first experience of real support she has had in years of violence. Yet because she has to rely on this man to represent her legal interests she has no choice but to comply with his wishes. This is a frustrating moment for the DVCS.

Crisis workers are particularly likely to find themselves in a conflict situation prior to a return hearing. The return hearing typically involves a contest between, on the one hand, the woman and her solicitor, wanting the interim order confirmed for twelve months and, on the other, the perpetrator and his solicitor, wanting the interim order cancelled. There will usually be a conference between these parties beforehand to see if some compromise agreement can be reached which can then be put to the court for approval. If the perpetrator is represented, he and his solicitor will be in one room and the woman and her solicitor, together with a crisis worker, will be in another. The negotiation will be conducted by the solicitors going from one room to the other. There may well be pressure on her to accept some compromise, for example, that the man be allowed home again provided he promises to give up drinking, or by having the exclusion order apply only when he is drunk. The woman may already be feeling uneasy about having asserted her need for protection in the way she has, never having done so before. She may be feeling very guilty about having had the man excluded from 'his' house, and she may feel under a strong obligation to compromise, especially if the compromise has the support of her solicitor. On the other hand, the crisis worker will explain to her that there is no legal compulsion to compromise, that she is entitled to continue to place her own safety first and that she has a right to go to court asking that the original order be confirmed. These conflicting priorities in such a tense situation can sometimes lead solicitors to conclude that the DVCS worker is obstructing the process and preventing an agreement being reached.

Soon after its inception the DVCS asked for an opportunity to speak to members of the Law Society in order to clarify its role. The venue chosen by the Law Society was the Canberra Club, which at the time still refused to have women as full members. The meeting was attended by about 45 lawyers. The intention was to review the new legislation and to describe the operations of the DVCS, but the meeting turned into an audience attack on the crisis service. Crisis workers were accused of being biased in favour of women, of wanting to deny perpetrators their civil rights and of interfering in the work of solicitors. There was also a general assumption in the room that the crisis workers were unqualified and it was clear that many of those present did not concede crisis workers any professional credibility and regarded them as akin to volunteer community workers. Finally, their remarks revealed that some of these lawyers had little respect for their female clients and shared all the assumptions of the wider society which, one way or another, blames women for their own victimisation.

LEGAL AID

Most of the women who apply for interim orders are eligible for the services of the Legal Aid Office. No means test for the receipt of legal aid is required at this stage, in order that the procedure for obtaining an interim order may be as streamlined as possible. However, applicants for orders are means tested prior to the return hearing and some women are required to seek private legal representation for their second hearing. The Legal Aid Office provides for the attendance of a domestic violence duty solicitor at the Magistrate's Court to deal with protection order applications. Legal Aid has made a considerable effort to staff this position sensitively, and it has generally been filled by a female solicitor, concerned about the safety of women victims.

Relations between the Legal Aid Office and the DVCS are excellent, and the duty solicitor has generally worked in very close cooperation with crisis workers. Legal Aid staff are thoroughly supportive of the DVCS, its role and its workers. They are also very receptive to suggestions about how the process might be improved and very willing to discuss problems which arise.

The workload of the Legal Aid Office has increased substantially since the legislation providing for domestic violence orders came into effect in 1986. In 1987–88 it handled about 300 applications for protection orders. All this was accomplished without any additional staff; the domestic violence duty solicitor, who began work at the court in 1987, had to be provided at the expense of other work done by the office. The advent of the DVCS in 1988 removed some the pressure from the duty solicitor since DVCS workers are able to assist with applications. But the activities of DVCS, coupled with the advertising it has done, have increased even further the number of women applying for orders, and the duty solicitor is now regularly overworked. The workload is manageable only because duty solicitors have had a personal commitment to respond effectively to the needs of victims of violence and are prepared routinely to work long hours. Not surprisingly, they are prone to 'burn out'and have to be rotated every six months or so. The Legal Aid Office has complained to government about this lack of resources and the DVCS has lobbied hard for increased government support in this area. In late 1990 some additional funds were forthcoming, but the lack of adequate funding for this work remains a serious problem, not only for the Legal Aid Office, but also for the DVCS and the staff of the court, not to mention the victims of violence themselves.

DIRECTOR OF PUBLIC PROSECUTIONS

The office of the Director of Public Prosections (DPP) is another section of the legal system with which the DVCS sometimes comes in contact. When a perpetrator is to be charged with assault, or some other criminal offence, it is the DPP which conducts the prosecution, on the basis of a brief provided by the police. Like Legal Aid, the DPP is seriously under-resourced, and this makes it impossible for it to devote adequate attention to these cases. The workload of prosecutors is such they sometimes find themselves preparing cases just minutes before a hearing. They may even be in the position of reading the file for the first time as they present the matter to the court. A domestic assault may be just one of several matters which the prosecutor has to deal with during the day, and no real consideration can be given to the particular circumstances of the case. In contrast, the perpetrator may have had extensive consultations with his solicitor who will be well prepared to fight the case.

Take, for example, an application for bail made by a man charged with assaulting his wife. The prosecutor may be unaware that the man has previously breached a domestic violence order or that he has previously assaulted his wife but not been charged with an offence. Neither he nor the police may know that on this occasion the man is threatening to kill his wife as soon as he is released. The prosecutor may thus be quite unaware of how vital it is for the woman that bail be opposed. All these circumstances will be known to the DVCS, because of its involvement with the woman prior to the hearing.

To deal with this problem, the DVCS set up lines of communication with the DPP, soon after the service was established. If such a case comes up now and the DVCS has some prior knowledge of it, it will advise the DPP in advance and stress how important it is to the woman that the man not be released on bail. The DPP is thus in a much better position to deal with the matter when it arises in court, though it is still unfortunately rare for bail to be denied.

The communication which now occurs between the DPP and the DVCS has also meant that that DPP has been able to call DVCS workers as expert witnesses in sentencing hearings. Thus the good working relationship between these two organisations has been very much to the advantage of battered women.

ADULT CORRECTIONS

A final government agency whose work is directly relevant to the work of the DVCS is Adult Corrective Services. One of its functions is to make recommendations to magistrates about sentences to be imposed on convicted offenders, including perpetrators of domestic violence. Among the possible options is the community service order, which can only be imposed as an alternative to imprisonment. But to allow a convicted perpetrator straight back into the home, or even into the community, is often to place the victim in immediate danger, and in these cases a community service order, or any other non-custodial sentence, is inappropriate. For these reasons Adult Corrections normally recommends against community service orders in the case of perpetrators of domestic violence. For an agency which is concerned about the rehabilitation of offenders, which treats offenders as 'clients' and which has traditionally taken the view that prison should be used only as a last resort, this is a very far-sighted stance. It is also a courageous stance because magistrates bend over backwards to keep offenders out of prison and frequently ignore these recommendations, choosing instead to impose community service orders.

Prior to the advent of the DVCS, Adult Corrections was not readily in a position to know the women's side of the story or to support its recommendation with much detail about the likely effect of a non-custodial sentence on the victim. However, the DVCS has established a close working relationship with the staff at Adult Corrections and is able to provide input into this process. This has been of assistance to Adult Corrections in recommending the incarceration of domestic violence offenders. Contact with this agency has thus been invaluable for the DVCS in its efforts to ensure safety for victims of violence.

COURT ACTION AGAINST VICTIMS OF VIOLENCE

Victims of violence can sometimes find themselves being criticised, threatened and even punished by the court. In what follows we provide some illustrative cases.

A woman had been terrorised for several years by a man. He had beaten her, threatened her with a gun and threatened to kill her child. She had relocated herself several times, but each time he managed to find her and continue his reign of terror. She reached the conclusion that the best way to stay alive was to appease him by living with him. There followed the worst beating of all after which he choked her, almost to death. A neighbour who heard this attack called the police and he was arrested and held in custody.

The man was a successful businessman and could afford a good lawyer. He had no prior criminal record and had professional colleagues prepared to testify on his behalf. Accordingly, the magistrate released him on bail, on the condition that he not approach the woman or her address. The DVCS did not expect him to observe this condition and so relocated the woman, yet again, to a secret address. The woman told nobody except a close friend. The man bribed or intimidated the friend into revealing the address and the next night, he arrived at her house, smashed down the front door, smashed a window, smashed the telephone, beat her up and left, saying, 'Next time you see me it will be the last time you see anybody' and, more significantly in the present context, 'If I get locked up, you are dead'.

In view of these threats the woman was not prepared voluntarily to give evidence against him. She feared for her life if she did. She was therefore subpoenaed by the prosecution.

When she appeared in court, very much against her will, she was paralysed with fear. There, in front of her, was the man who was threatening to kill her if she gave evidence against him. She refused to answer questions. The magistrate thereupon threatened to put her 'down in the cells' immediately for refusing to cooperate with the court, and told her he could incarcerate her for eight days if need be. He then adjourned the court for ten minutes to give her time to reconsider. This threat was partially successful; when he returned she reluctantly, fearfully and, with a great deal of under-statement and even fabrication, told an unconvincing and watered down version of the story. The defendant's lawyer was jubilant. The prosecutor, in despair, declared the woman a hostile witness because he knew that the magistrate regarded her behaviour as offensive to the court and that it was working in favour of the defendant. The police felt that the woman had let them down. Nobody understood. Nobody realised just how terrified the woman was. Caught between the death threats of the perpetrator and the magistrate's threat to imprison her, she was trapped.

A second way in which the legal system sometimes works against the victims of violence is by charging them with aiding and abet-ting the breach of a domestic violence order. In one such case a woman who had an exclusion order in force against a man had allowed him to enter her house when he asked to talk to her about reconciliation. He assaulted her severely, threatened her with fur-ther violence and threatened to hurt her children. She called the police, who arrested the man for assault and for trespass. They then discovered that there was an order in place. Accordingly, the assault charge was reduced to breaching the order and the woman was charged with aiding and abetting his breach by having allowed him into the house. The DVCS intervened in this process and made representations to the police and the DPP, seeking under-standing for the woman's actions, but to no avail. The man was fined $200 for his breach. She was found guilty and given a com-munity service order. Community service can only be ordered as an alternative to imprisonment, that is, when a defendant would otherwise be sent to prison. Thus, in imposing the sentences it did, the court appeared to be suggesting that her offence was more serious than his.

One final example of the way in which victims of violence have sometimes fallen foul of the court is worth recounting. A woman who had thrown an object at her ex-husband was in court on an assault charge. She became incensed at the story the prosecutor was presenting to the court, and shouted out to the magistrate that it was all lies. She interrupted proceedings on several occasions, and tried to have everyone listen to her stories of the ex-husband's violence and what she had been through over several years. She was asked several times to refrain from her interruptions. Finally, she made an angry threat that if her ex-husband did anything to hurt her children she would kill him. She was thereupon held to be in contempt of court and the magistrate ordered that she be taken into custody, where she was held for five days. Her offence was not that she had made a death threat— violent men do that regularly and, even though witnesses may testify to the threats, they are not regarded as serious enough in themselves to warrant punishment. Her offence was to have made the threat in court and it was for this that she was punished.

THE BAIL QUESTION: VICTIMS' VERSUS PERPETRATORS' INTERESTS

When a perpetrator is arrested on an assault charge, and assuming that the police do not themselves release him on bail, he has a right to go before a magistrate as soon as practicable to request bail. If the police fear that the man is likely to assault the woman in retaliation for calling the police, they will oppose bail at this stage. There is some doubt about the law on this point, but on one view magistrates are entitled to take account of the consequences for the victim entailed by the perpetrator's release, particularly as the victim is a potential witness whom the perpetrator may try to intimidate. On this view magistrates are in a position to deny the bail application if they believe that the risk of further violence is significant. Be that as it may, the courts are usually unwilling to deprive accused persons of their liberty and often release perpetrators, despite police requests. In this respect the legal system tends to place the interests of perpetrators ahead of the interests of victims.

A magistrate may impose bail conditions; for example, that the man not go near the woman he is alleged to have assaulted. But this affords the woman no real protection, for where a perpetrator is determined to retaliate he is quite prepared to breach the conditions. If he is re-arrested for such a breach and comes before the court again on a bail application, magistrates are much more likely this second time round to deny bail, on the grounds that the bail conditions were breached. The court sometimes appears more influenced by a breach of bail conditions than by the history of previous violence which lead police to oppose bail in the first place. In these circumstances the court appears to respond more decisively to an offence against itself than to the crime of assault.

If the magistrate decides to release a perpetrator on bail, it is vital that the DVCS be aware of this so that the woman can be taken into hiding, if there are any fears for her safety. Sometimes, however, the DVCS fails to get the information in time. In one case, where the perpetrator was released on condition that he not approach the woman, by the time the information came through, the man had been to her house and assaulted her, she had rung the police and he had disappeared.

Just before this book went to press a Canberra man killed his wife and two children and then himself. Earlier that day he had been before the court for breaching a domestic violence order. Despite police opposition, the magistrate had released him on bail. Until the courts are prepared to give precedence to the safety of victims rather than the civil rights of perpetrators in these circumstances, such atrocities will continue and no amount of law reform can prevent them. The movement against domestic violence still has a long way to go.

PROMOTING CHANGE IN THE LEGAL SYSTEM

It is clear from what we have said that the legal system as a whole is not sufficiently understanding of the situation of victims of domestic violence. In an attempt to promote better understanding, some two years after it began operation the DVCS organised a 'legal forum'—a panel consisting of the chief magistrate and one other magistrate, two police officers, legal aid and private lawyers, and representatives of other parts of the legal system. It is a tribute to the commitment and concern of these people that they were so willing to cooperate in this exercise. The panel was asked to discuss the response of the legal system to domestic violence, before an audience of 200. Imaginary scenarios were put to panel members who were invited to say how they would respond in their official capacity. They were also asked to imagine they were playing the roles of others in the drama. In the process, the inadequacies of the system response were manifest to all.

Two particular conclusions emerged from this role-playing activity. First, those who were asked to imagine themselves as the victim reported that none of the advice and assistance they were receiving really helped them to deal with the immediate crisis and they remained confused and frightened. Second, while the real police officers exhibited great caution in arresting perpetrators, magistrates and lawyers who were asked to play the police role seemed more willing to arrest perpetrators, even if there was insufficient evidence to be sure of winning in court. The overriding consideration seemed to be that the perpetrator's behaviour was unacceptable and the legal system needed to respond accordingly.

Whether this exercise resulted in any real change in thinking is hard to say. Perhaps the most significant achievement of the forum was to symbolise to those present, who included the ACT's Attorney-General, the importance which the community is now attaching to the problem of domestic violence, and to alert them to the fact that the legal system is being scrutinised for the adequacy of its response. The forum was an innovative attempt by the DVCS to act as a catalyst for change.

CONCLUSION

The response of the legal system is critical to the protection of victims of violence. The law itself is progressive in this area, but its application continues to be hampered by inadequate resources, by certain aspects of legal ideology and practice, and above all, by an inadequate understanding of domestic violence on the part of some legal system personnel. The DVCS has sometimes found itself frustrated by these problems in its attempts to help women seeking legal protection from violence. Change is essential if domestic violence is to be effectively curtailed and it is for this reason that the DVCS is not only using the legal system but promoting its improvement.

9   Violence in the home as crime

Assaulting women in the home is undoubtedly a criminal offence. The aim of the movement against domestic violence has been to get the police, the courts and, more generally, society to treat it as such. Previous chapters have sought to describe and explain the movement. In the present chapter, we hope to contribute more directly to this movement by arguing for the appropriateness of treating domestic violence as criminal and the inappropriateness of certain alternative approaches. As a preliminary point, however, it is important to note that there is a sense in which recently enacted law reforms have been in the reverse direction.

THE IRONY OF LAW REFORM

Law reform has been an integral feature of the movement against domestic violence and has, we would argue, provided the police with more effective legal tools for use against crime of this nature. In particular, police powers of entry have been strengthened and victims have been made compellable witnesses, thus increasing the chance of conviction once a matter goes to court. The irony is, however, that the domestic violence orders, which are the centrepiece of most new legislation, are essentially non-criminal in nature (see Chapter 6). In this sense law reform has decriminalised domestic violence. Jocelynne Scutt has written critically of this development, describing it as 'going backwards'. She makes the point very clearly in an interview for *Australian Society* (1986: 27):

> If a woman's been bashed up, my position is that police have the power to go onto the property. They have the power to arrest, and that's what they should be doing. *Now* [with the advent of domestic violence orders], if a woman's bashed, police don't arrest, apparently they take out an intervention order [or suggest that the woman do so]. The next time she rings and says 'he's round again and bashed me again', we're expected to believe the police come back and arrest the man. First of all, the woman has suffered two crimes. [Second], if the man is arrested, he's not being arrested for a crime, he's being arrested because he's breached an intervention order which is an insult to the court; he's in contempt of court. What is actually being said by that procedure is

114

that it's far worse for a man to insult the court, a male institution, than for a man to bash up a woman.

Scutt's point is a good one. We, too, would like to see the police making far greater use of their powers of arrest, and we shall argue shortly that this would be likely to have a significant effect on the incidence of domestic violence. Nevertheless, the fact is that the police are unwilling to arrest perpetrators, for a variety of both practical and ideological reasons (see chapter 7). Domestic violence orders, on the other hand, are being used routinely and, as a practical matter, women are receiving greater protection from the legal system than previously. In these circumstances we believe the new law to be a step forwards, not backwards, as Scutt suggests. (For a fuller discussion of the rationale for domestic violence orders see Seddon, 1986.)

APPROACHES TO DOMESTIC VIOLENCE

In what follows we shall first discuss two popular approaches which tend to minimise the criminal nature of domestic violence. The first sees the violence as being associated with alcohol consumption, which diminishes the perpetrator's responsibility for his behaviour. The second, very much in vogue as we write, sees domestic violence as an expression of marital conflict, for which conflict resolution is the appropriate response. After criticising these approaches we shall argue for the appropriateness of treating domestic violence as crime, and suggest that such an approach is likely to have a significant impact on the problem.

THE ALCOHOL EXCUSE

It is a widely held view that much domestic violence occurs at a time when the perpetrator is drunk and that the alcohol is really the source of the problem. Police, victims and perpetrators all, at times, express this view. 'If only we could dry these blokes out, we'd stop domestics,' say the police. 'He's as gentle as a lamb when he's sober,' says many a victim. Even the perpetrator excuses himself with: 'It's the grog that does it.' On this view the perpetrator is not regarded as being fully responsible for his behaviour, and criminal prosecution is seen to be an unnecessarily heavy-handed approach.

There are several problems with this explanation (McGregor, 1990b). First, many acts of violence are committed by men who have not been drinking—perhaps 50 per cent (Queensland Task Force, 1988: 39)—and there are many men who drink but don't beat their wives. Moreover, some men who beat their wives when drunk do so when sober as well. Alcohol consumption is thus neither a necessary nor a sufficient condition for violence to occur.

Furthermore, research to date has failed to show even a statistical association between alcohol and domestic violence (see Weatherburn, 1990). Almost all research on the subject examines populations of perpetrators and shows that a certain proportion of them had been drinking at the time of the offence. But such data can tell us nothing about the relationship between alcohol and violence. Valid inferences depend on comparing the rates of violence of alcohol consumers and non-alcohol consumers.

Let us make the point more concretely. Assume that 50 per cent of batterers have been drinking at the time of the offence. But suppose, also, that at the time when much domestic violence occurs, namely in the evenings, 50 per cent of non-batterers are also drinking—a plausible supposition. We would then conclude that there was no association between drinking and violence. To our knowledge it has not in fact been shown that drinkers are disproportionately prone to beat their wives.

Of course it may be that in individual cases there is an association between alcohol and violence, in that the violence occurs only or largely when the perpetrator has been drinking. Alcohol in these cases may function as a disinhibiter, or a 'trigger' for violence. However, the fact that for so many men and women it does not act as a trigger in this way casts further doubt on the causal significance of the alcohol.

A second major problem with the alcohol excuse is that there is good reason to think that men who beat their wives when drunk are fully aware of what they are doing. They avoid hitting their partners in front of other people. They often have the presence of mind to beat a woman where it will not show. Some men even get drunk with the intention of beating their wives while intoxicated. All such men are making choices and can reasonably be held responsible for their behaviour.

It is important to note that the law does not automatically assume that intoxication renders an offender less responsible for his actions. We shall discuss this point in some detail in what follows because it is widely and mistakenly believed that legal considerations necessitate a more lenient response to an offender who is drunk. We shall refer to both English and Australian law since Australian judges almost invariably discuss the English precedents in making Australian law, although they do not necessarily follow them.

Intoxication can be relevant in two ways. Generally speaking, to be guilty of an offence, a person must not only commit the prohibited act but must also have done so in a culpable fashion. If the act was committed unintentionally then, broadly speaking, the defendant is not guilty. The second way in which intoxication can be relevant is in determining the severity of the sentence, once a person has been found guilty. At this stage, drunkenness may sometimes be regarded as a mitigating factor, resulting in a reduced sentence. But it may also be treated as an aggravating factor, with the opposite effect.

On the question of guilt, the law in England explicitly rejects intoxication as a defence in assault cases. A man who had assaulted the landlord and customers at a pub and subsequently assaulted police sought to defend himself on the grounds that he was drunk and had not intended to commit the assaults. The matter was finally decided in an appeal to the House of Lords, which rejected his defence. The reasoning was as follows:

> One of the prime purposes of the criminal law, with its penal sanctions, is protection from certain proscribed conduct of persons who are pursuing their lawful lives. Unprovoked violence has, from time immemorial, been a significant part of such proscribed conduct. To accede to the argument on behalf of the appellant would leave the citizen legally unprotected from unprovoked violence, where such violence was the consequence of drink or drugs having obliterated the capacity of the perpetrator to know what he was doing or what were its consequences (Brett et al. 1989: 745)

In Australian law, intoxication is not completely ruled out as a possible defence in this way, but it is relevant only in exceptional cases where the defendant can prove that he was so drunk that he was not aware of what he was doing. The mere fact that he cannot remember the incident is *not* evidence that his action was unintentional. Nor is the fact that he would not have committed the offence while sober (Brett, 1989: 764). Thus, in the great majority of domestic assaults committed while under the influence of alcohol, Australian law holds the perpetrator guilty (see also Goode, 1985).

As for sentencing, matters are somewhat confused. In England the Court of Appeal usually rejects alcohol as a reason for reducing sentences, although judges in the lower courts sometimes take it into account (Walker, 1985: 48). In Australia, intoxication may be treated as a mitigating factor, provided the court is satisfied that the behaviour is out of character and unlikely to be repeated. Neither of these things is true for most perpetrators of domestic violence. But even where the defendant is otherwise of good character, intoxication will not necessarily be accepted as a mitigating factor. Here are the words of a South Australian chief justice:

> ...there are offences in which, as it seems to me, the deterrent purpose

of punishment must take priority. When people act under the influence of liquor, passion, anger or the like so as to constitute themselves a physical danger or potential physical danger to other citizens it may well be that a sentence of imprisonment will be appropriate even in the case of a first offender of good character, in order to impress on the community at large that such behaviour will not be tolerated. (Quoted in Fox and Freiberg, 1985: 472)

Finally, alcohol can be an aggravating factor in sentencing. For offences such as driving under the influence, the greater the intoxication the more severe the sentence. Likewise, alcohol is an aggravating factor in relation to the offence of causing death by culpable driving (Fox and Freiberg, 1985: 472, 503).

It is clear from this discussion that the law does not normally regard intoxication as a reason for dealing more leniently with violent assaults, domestic or otherwise. The widespread prejudice in the community on this point in favour of perpetrators of domestic violence, a prejudice shared unfortunately by some members the legal and law enforcement professions, is not supported by the criminal law itself. Those who wish to excuse drunken perpetrators on the grounds that they are not responsible for their behaviour are defying the undoubted wisdom of the criminal law in this respect.

VIOLENCE AND CONFLICT

One of the complaints made time and again by police about the activities of the DVCS is that it invariably takes the side of the woman in the 'dispute' and that it does not seem to be interested in promoting a 'reconciliation' between the parties. This complaint reflects a view, widespread among the police and the community, that domestic violence is an outcome of conflict and that some form of 'conflict resolution' is an appropriate response to assault in the home. Various mediation and conflict resolution services have emerged in Australia in recent years and all believe that they have some role to play in cases of domestic violence. Even the National Women's Consultative Council, which describes itself as 'the federal government's principal mechanism for consulting with women in the community', views conflict resolution as a strategy worth exploring in the the context of domestic violence.

A major problem with this approach is that, as in the case of alcohol, much violence occurs in the absence of any conflict. This is especially true in chronic cases of wife battering (McGregor, 1990a). Many women survivors of violence report that in the period leading up to a violent attack by the male partner there was no conflict between them. Indeed, women often go to great lengths to remove all sources of conflict they perceive in the relationship.

They will try to cook better meals, stay awake for him no matter what time he gets home, have sex with him whenever he wants, have the children in bed before he gets home, have the house immaculate, lose weight, get a job, give up a job, give up friendships, keep thoughts and opinions private, sever relations with their family of origin, move house, move town and suggest counselling. Women often do everything in their power to appease their partner. Yet the violence continues.

One of the more common triggers to violence is a woman's failure to have the meal on the table at the prescribed time. This is a particularly revealing case because often in these circumstances there is very clearly no confict. There is, in fact, explicit agreement, since the woman accepts that it is her duty to have his dinner ready at the appointed time and acknowledges that she has, for whatever reason, failed in her duty. The violence in these circumstances is simply punishment for non-compliance.

If, on the other hand, such a woman does not accept her partner's definition of her domestic responsibilities, there is indeed a conflict, but the violence remains a means of punishing her for defying his rules rather than a tactic for resolving conflict. Any intervention aimed at resolving the conflict over her role misses the point. The violence in this case stems from his presumed right to punish her, and it is this which must be addressed in any intervention. Unless his presumed right to punish her is challenged directly, the resolution of any particular conflict will do nothing to end the violence, because there will always be other behaviour of hers which in his view warrants punishment.

This last point is not sufficiently appreciated by the proponents of the conflict resolution approach. Admittedly, such services usually take the view that violence of any form is unacceptable, that violence is the responsibility of the perpetrator and that the cessation of violence is non-negotiable. But they are nevertheless prepared to mediate in conflicts which the parties themselves believe contribute to the violence (Hazlehurst, 1989: 4). Such a strategy not only does not get to the root cause of the violence, but it subtly implicates the victim, in that it implies that some compromise on her part may reduce the likelihood of violence.

The idea that violence constitutes punishment in the eyes of the perpetrator may need some further elaboration. The fact is that the explanations which a perpetrator offers for his behaviour are multiple. Sometimes he will blame the alcohol and claim that he was not responsible for his behaviour. Sometimes he will claim that her behaviour so enraged him that he was driven to violence—again, a denial of responsibility. But often, along with such claims, will be the justification that she 'asked' for it, that she 'deserved' it. This formulation is very revealing of the thinking which underlies the resort to violence. The concept of desert is inextricably linked to that of punishment. Desert is the most fundamental and primitive of humanity's justifications for punishment, long preceding such justifications as deterrence, rehabilitation or incapacitation. Thus, in claiming that she 'deserved' it, the perpetrator is in effect claiming that she has transgressed his rules and that his violent behaviour is her punishment.

Another way to bring out the inappropriateness of viewing domestic violence as conflict is to compare the beating which a man might give to a child who irritates or defies him with the equivalent beating he might administer to his wife who has similarly irritated or defied him. Violence by a parent against a child is seen either as legitimate punishment, or as child abuse, depending on the circumstances and on one's values. There is little tendency to conceptualise such violence as conflict. Yet when the recipient of the violence is an adult that is exactly how it is often seen. We would argue, however, that the interpersonal dynamics are essentially the same.

Violent assaults by men against their female partners often occur after the relationship has ended and when the woman is trying to separate. While it might be argued that this is a situation of conflict (she wants to go; he wants her to stay), we believe such a conceptualisation to be profoundly inappropriate. A woman who has decided to leave a relationship has every right to do so and, assuming she is clear about her decision, it should not be treated as a dispute to be resolved. A man's violence in these circumstances is simply an exercise of power designed to force her to stay or to punish her for leaving.

It is also relevant to note here that for no other crime does the criminal justice system see dispute resolution between the offender and the victim as the appropriate strategy. Although in the case of a burglary there is a dispute (the burglar wants the homeowner's possessions and the homeowner wishes to retain them), the law treats burglary as a crime to be punished rather than a dispute to be resolved. It might be objected that this is an unfair comparison since in cases of domestic assault there is a pre-existing relationship, absent in the case of burglary. Consider, therefore, the case of embezzlement. Such as offence presupposes a pre-existing relationship between an employer and a trusted employee. Even so, the law has no hesitation in treating such an occurrence as a criminal offence rather than as a dispute.

A final objection to the view that violence is the outcome of conflict is that conflict occurs in many situations without consequent violence. A man may experience extreme conflict at work with his boss, but not resort to violence. Yet the same man may beat his wife during an argument. If conflict is followed by violence in one relationship but not in another, then conflict cannot be the source of the violence.

Although we have been critical of the conflict resolution approach where violence is involved, we acknowledge that there are many circumstances where it can be usefully applied. But in identifying those circumstances it is crucial that violence not be confused with conflict. Conflict is about argument and disagreement. Violence is the abuse of power—behaviour which results in a less powerful person being physically or psychologically damaged. Conflict resolution is useful when there is equality between the parties, as for example in disputes between neighbours. In relations between men and women, where conflict usually takes place against a backdrop of gender inequality, conflict resolution strategies will often be to the detriment of the less powerful.

As usual, Scutt puts the point well in her critique of the contemporary trend towards community-based mediation (1988: 516):

> The implication that disputes can best be resolved by mediation, conciliation, and counselling ignores power differentials and inequality. The idea that the problems of the adversary system and traditional justice can be resolved by the establishment of alternative systems hides from view the fact that despite valid criticisms of the adversarial process, positive aspects exist which should not be removed from disadvantaged groups in particular.
>
> ...The privatisation of justice is detrimental to the interests of the disadvantaged, in that it shuts off from public view the very nature of the inequality from which the individual and group suffers. Whilst the feminist movement is fighting for recognition amongst all women of abuses committed against women as members of a group, 'private justice' is fighting back to individualise those abuses. 'Private justice' renders the personal apolitical.

PATRIARCHAL BELIEFS

In our view male violence is an outcome of the social processes by which masculinity is constructed (Connell, 1987: 183); it stems from traditions, habits and beliefs about what it is to be a man (Jenkins, 1990: 38). There are two particular beliefs involved. First, the belief that men have a right to exercise authority over their partners—a right to deference and obedience from the women they live with. The second, related belief is that violence is a legitimate form of punishment which may be used in the exercise of this authority.

This is clearly a controversial position and one which, if

accepted, has far-reaching policy implications. How is it to be defended?

Let us begin by noting that the patriarchal belief system described above was explicitly built into the law until recent times. Here are the words of an eighteenth-century English legal text (quoted in Edwards, 1985: 189): 'For as [the husband] is to answer for "misbehaviour" [of the wife], the law thought it reasonable to instruct him with this power of chastisement in the same moderation that a man is allowed to correct his apprentices and children.' A nineteeth-century text explains that a man charged with assaulting his wife could defend himself by arguing that his violence was punishment, for example, 'a bell not answered with the required promptitude—a dinner somewhat late or badly cooked—a pair of slippers not to be found when wanted—a book carried off—a set of papers disarranged' (quoted in Edwards, 1985: 190).

It was not until 1891 that the English law did away with a husband's right to beat his wife (Scutt, 1986: 49). Even so, lower courts still occasionally asserted a man's right to chastise his wife. As recently as 1946 the English Court of Appeal overturned a decision of a lower court which had held that a domestic assault was legitimate punishment for a wife who had disobeyed her husband by visiting her relatives (Stratmann, 1982: 120).

The law no longer sees wife assault as a legitimate exercise of male authority. But it is only 100 years since this belief system was so widespread that it was part of the law of the land. The written law can change overnight, but belief systems are far more entrenched. Our point is simply that it would be astonishing if the beliefs discernable in the law until such recent times were not still present in significant sections of present day society.

Confirmation of this view was provided by the 1988 attitude survey commissioned by the Office of the Status of Women. The survey found that one in five people believe that the use of physical force by a man against his wife is acceptable in some circumstances. These respondents believed that it might be justifiable for a man to shove, kick or hit his wife if she did not obey him, wasted money, was a sloppy housekeeper or refused him sex. These people, in short, believe that a man has a right to use violence to punish his partner if she in some way defies his presumed authority.

Our second argument in support of the explanation of male violence in terms of patriarchal beliefs begins with the observation that none of the other suggested causes—alcohol, conflict, unemployment, stress—necessarily leads to violence; nor are they necessarily present when violence does occur. Many of the most commonly cited 'causes' have not even been convincingly shown to correlate with violence, as we discussed in some detail in the case of alcohol. (The evidence for these assertions is presented in the Queensland Task Force Report, chapters 2 and 4).

The point is this: if we are seeking to reduce the incidence of domestic violence, then government policies aimed at eliminating these 'causes' are not likely to have a major impact on the problem. And this is quite apart from the question of whether governments are capable or even desirous of eliminating unemployment, alcohol consumption, stress or any other presumed cause.

In contrast to the factors just discussed, the belief that violence is a legitimate means of exercising authority is normally present in men who beat their partners and absent in men who don't. Let us focus on the first and more controversial part of this claim, namely, that perpetrators normally feel justified in what they do.

Surely, one might think, perpetrators who beat their partners in anger do not necessarily believe in the legitimacy of their behaviour. Indeed, many of them subsequently express remorse, suggesting that they believe their violence to have been unjustified. However, such remorse is occasioned not by the violence but the fear that the partner may leave. Perpetrators will often put considerable energy into apologising to their partners in order to avoid such an outcome. Furthermore, even perpetrators who beat their partners in anger often admit that they were not really out of control (Elliot and Shanahan, 1988). The fact is that perpetrator anger is self-righteous anger ('how dare she behave in such and such a way') and violence in these circumstances is clearly punishment. Such punishment may be for her failure to comply with his expectations or, more generally, for challenging in some way the right he presumes to deference and obedience from his female partner.

The belief in the legitimacy of violence as a technique for controlling the behaviour of female partners is, as we have said, an aspect of the patriarchal ideology which permeates society. Patriarchal ideology is inculcated into men by the media and by peer group and family socialisation. Of course, the processes of socialisation are not uniform and not all men are bearers of these beliefs to the same degree. Moreover, there are also countervailing socialisation processes at work. Thus, many men do not engage in violence against their partners.

Although it is not part of the argument here, we note in passing that violence by parents against children is based on a very similar belief system, namely, that parents have a right to exercise authority over children and that it is legitimate to resort to physical punishment in the exercise of this authority. Violence by women against men, on the other hand, is a very different phenomenon. It is not based on any assumed right to exercise authority over a male partner. In many cases it is simply a matter of self-defence. It is noteworthy that, in the USA, certain women charged with murdering their husbands have been acquitted, on that grounds that they acted in self-defence, even though their actions were premeditated. In one such case, a man, who had previously beaten his wife severely, went to sleep, promising to kill her when he awoke. She chose to kill him before he woke up, and the court subsequently accepted that she had acted in self-defence. (See Bograd, 1990, for a more complete discussion of the different meanings of male and female violence. See McNeely and Richey Mann, 1990, for a somewhat contrary view.)

The explanation of domestic violence in terms of a patriarchal belief system differs from most other explanations in that it avoids blaming or implicating the victim in any way. Most other analyses focus on the interaction of the perpetrator and the victim around the time of the violence and inevitably see the behaviour of the victim as contributing in some way to the violence, innocently triggering it, perhaps, or less innocently provoking it. Implicit in all such analyses is the view that had the victim behaved differently the violence would not have occurred. This view attributes at least some of the responsibility or blame for the violence to the victim. A patriarchal analysis, on the other hand, sees the violence as flowing from a choice made by the perpetrator. It insists that this choice is structured by the wider social context, not by the behaviour of the victim.

The claim that a belief in the legitimacy of violence is at the root of wife assault is hardly a profound claim from a conventional social science viewpoint. It does not, for example, enable us to indentify a category of men with particular life experiences or sociological or psychological characteristics who are prone to beat their wives. Nor does it predict the circumstances under which violence will occur. Indeed, it comes close to being a truism: people who behave in a certain way do so because they believe it appropriate to do so.

Nevertheless, it is a claim with profound policy consequences, for it implies that if we wish to change the behaviour we must first change the belief about the acceptability of the behaviour. There are various ways in which this might be attempted. Educational campaigns, for example, are a frequent government strategy in such circumstances, although the effectiveness of large-scale government advertising campaigns is open to some doubt (Morehead and Penman, 1989). Another often suggested tactic is the provision of counselling for perpetrators who wish it. But this presupposes that perperators wish to change their beliefs, a quite unrealistic assumption, given that they regard their behaviour as justified in the first place. We shall say more about this shortly. In our view, perpetrators' beliefs are most effectively changed by publicly confronting them with a clear, authoritative statement that their behaviour is socially unacceptable. The best way to make such a statement is by invoking the criminal law.

THE IMPACT OF THE CRIMINAL LAW

The application of the criminal law to an offender can promote law-abiding behaviour in that person in two different ways. First, the unpleasantness of the process may simply deter the person from further offences. Second, the process may generate in the offender a commitment to the moral principles inherent in the law. This is the moral-educative function of the law. To give just two examples of this latter process, first, it is generally accepted that the prohibition on price-fixing agreements among business competitors, coupled with the fact that some business executives in the USA have been sent to gaol for the practice, over time, has created a climate of business opinion in that country critical of price fixing (see generally Braithwaite and Geis, 1982: 300–05). Second, survey evidence in New South Wales indicates that as a result of the introduction and widespread application of random breath testing an increasing number of people are willing to label the drinking driver as 'irresponsible, a criminal or a potential murderer' (Hommel, 1990).

The deterrent and moral-educative functions of the law are, of course, closely related and in many situations where the application of the law has successfully prevented further offences it will be impossible to tell which of these two processes predominated. But a clever experiment by Schwartz and Orleans (1967) clearly demonstrated the distinction:

> Taxpayers were interviewed during the month prior to the filing of income tax returns, with one randomly selected group exposed to an interview stressing the penalties for income tax evasion, the other to an interview stressing the moral reasons for tax compliance. Whereas the moral appeal led to a significant increase in the actual tax paid, the deterrent threat was associated with no significant increase in tax paid compared to a control group. (Braithwaite, 1989: 70–1)

It is important to note that neither the deterrent nor the moral-educative effect of the criminal law necessarily depends on the application of a punishment; the mere fact of arrest or appearance in court is often enough:

> A British...survey asked youths to rank what they saw as the most

important consequence of arrest. While only 10 per cent said 'the punishment I might get' was the most important consequence of arrest, 55 per cent said either 'what my family' or 'my girlfriend' would think about it. Another 12 per cent ranked the 'publicity or shame of having to appear in court' as the most serious consequence of arrest. (Braithwaite, 1989: 70)

Thus, in arguing for the application of the criminal law to domestic violence offenders we are not necessarily arguing that they should be severely punished, although that may indeed be appropriate in some cases. The required deterrent and/or moral-educative effect may well be achieved by arrest alone.

Braithwaite's important recent work, *Crime, Shame and Reintegration,* allows us to take the discussion a stage further. He argues persuasively that the operations of the legal system will produce either or both of the required preventive effects only if the legal process successfully shames the offender. Shaming operates when the offender remains essentially a part of the wider moral community so that he or she is affected by the moral condemnation implied in the legal process. Shaming in these circumstances is morally educative: it promotes the internalisation of society's codes in the same way that children internalise the moral values of their parents. It is also a deterrent to further offending since the feeling of shame is very much an experience to be avoided. But to operate in this way the shaming must not be so great as to ostracise offenders irrevocably. Following shaming they must be reintegrated into the community of which they are members.

Let us consider some examples to clarify the process. Publicising corporate wrongdoing is a form of shaming which renders corporate executives exceedingly uncomfortable, even though the legal process may be focused on the company itself and not its personnel. It challenges their conception of themselves as law-abiding citizens. The result is that publicity is a very effective means of controlling corporate misconduct (Fisse and Brahwaite, 1983). On the other hand, members of a delinquent sub-culture are not shamed by criminal proceedings because they are alienated from the wider society and are supported in their deviant behaviour by sub-cultural values. The processes of the criminal law have no moral-educative effect on such people and very little deterrent effect. Indeed, punishment may simply embitter them and thus promote, rather than deter, further offences. One final example of the failure of legal proceedings to have any preventive effect when they fail to shame concerns the arrest and prosecution of environmental demonstrators. These people are powerfully insulated from shame by their belief in the rightness of their cause, and in these circumstances legal processes are quite incapable of promoting respect for, or even obedience to, the law.

It is our contention that the perpetrator of domestic violence is likely to be effectively shamed by experiencing the procedures of the criminal justice system. Unlike many delinquents who are members of supportive sub-cultures, the domestic violence offender is seldom supported by those around him. In fact he will usually seek to hide his behaviour from others. He frequently regards himself as a law-abiding citizen. Thus, to be confronted by the processes of the criminal law—arrest, prosecution and the like—all of which are making the statement that his behaviour is criminal, even that *he* is a criminal, will be an acutely uncomfortable, indeed shameful experience. It forcibly confronts him with the fact that in the eyes of significant sections of society, wife assault is unacceptable, and he will feel that if he wishes to remain an accepted member of that society he will have to accept its moral precepts.

In any case, it is not as if patriarchal instructions unambiguously condone domestic violence. While one strand of patriarchal ideology permits the physical disciplining of a wife, another holds that to hit a women is unchivalrous, even cowardly. In a sense, therefore, wife beating is a morally ambiguous activity, even for the perpetrator. The application of the criminal law in these circumstances may effectively increase the salience of one strand of patriarchal ideology at the expense of another.

All this is theory. Is there any real evidence that the use of the criminal justice system does indeed have a preventive effect on perpetrators? After all, there is a great deal of research showing that the arrest and punishment of most other offenders has little if any preventive effect. The answer is: yes. There is now a body of research which clearly demonstrates the preventive effects of arrest on perpetrators of domestic violence. We outline the findings below. Nothing to our knowledge has yet been published about the effects of conviction or formal punishment.

The most famous and influential of the studies on the effect of arrest on perpetrators is the Minneapolis experiment. Over the course of eighteen months police were called to deal with over 300 domestic assaults where arrest was legally possible. Approximately half the offenders, randomly chosen, were arrested while the remainder were counselled or ordered to stay away from the victim for eight hours. The researchers found that those arrested were substantially less likely than the others to come to police attention again for domestic violence in a six-month period following the police intervention. Furthermore, interviews with victims during this period confirmed that perpetrators who had been arrested were less prone to commit further acts of violence than those not arrested. Various objections have been raised to the generalisability of the findings, but despite these objections, the results have so impressed police departments across the USA that many have now changed their domestic violence arrest policies from 'officer discretion' to 'encouragement of arrest' (Sherman et al., 1986: 167).

A second study (Berk and Newton, 1985) of 783 wife batterers in California came to the same conclusion, namely that those arrested were less likely to re-offend than those not arrested. Futhermore, among offenders who for other reasons were thought to be highly likely to re-offend, 65 per cent of those not arrested did in fact come to police attention for a further act of wife beating while the comparable figure for those arrested was only 25 per cent. Finally, a Canadian study (Jaffe et al., 1986) found a significant reduction in victim-reported violence following police intervention, especially when charges were laid. What these studies all suggest is that whether or not charges are followed by successful prosecution, arrest has a demonstrable effect in preventing further occurrences of domestic violence.

But the matter is not yet settled. The research community has expressed some scepticism about these findings and a series of replications of the Minneapolis experiment have been funded by the US National Institute of Justice. At the time of writing, the findings of one of these—the Omaha police experiment—have been published (Dunford et al., 1990). The results were somewhat inconsistent, but did show quite clearly that victims reported fewer cases of violence and longer periods free from violence after perpetrators had been arrested, as compared with cases where the perpetrators had been informally removed or counselled by police. However, using the conservative statistical criterion that differences are only regarded as significant if one can be 95 per cent certain that they did not occur by chance, the authors concluded that there was no significant difference between arrest and non-arrest in deterring further offences.

On balance, then, the research results to date suggest that arrest does have an appreciable effect. In this respect, violence in the home is unlike most other crime. It is closest, in fact, to white-collar crime in its deterrability by criminal justice procedures.

It would seem, therefore, that Australian police forces should be encouraged to make far greater use of arrest in cases of domestic assault than they currently do. Australian police are often reluctant to arrest in view of the difficulties in obtaining a conviction in such cases. It is often the word of the perpetrator against that of the victim, and judges are legally obliged to give the defendant the benefit of any such doubt. Moreover, for reasons discussed earlier, victims are often unreliable witnesses. The police are thus understandably hesitant to prosecute, fearing that cases will be lost for lack of evidence and that they will be made to appear foolish in the process. However, it would seem on the basis of the research findings that a realistic policy for the police to adopt is to arrest perpetrators and then drop the charges as soon as it becomes clear that the evidence will be difficult to obtain. The police resist such a policy for fear that it might lay them open to accusations of false arrest. But in the policing of political demonstrations, particularly environmental protests, large numbers of charges are routinely laid and subsequently dropped, without the question of false arrest arising. Police fears in this respect would therefore appear to be exaggerated.

We are not, of course, arguing that there is no need to proceed to the conviction and punishment of perpetrators. There are many situations in which what is called for is a long period of incarceration, in order to incapacitate offenders, that is, to physically prevent them from re-offending. What we are saying is simply that the shaming potential of the criminal justice system is not being used to its full capacity in domestic violence cases.

Nor do we wish to deny the possible value of various rehabilitative strategies. However, one such strategy which is currently being promoted, perpetrator counselling, needs to be treated with extreme caution. Counselling for violent men should not be seen as an alternative to arrest and conviction, for the reasons mentioned earlier. It should follow a formal finding of guilt which makes it clear to the offender that his behaviour is criminal. It should be aimed at helping the offender to avoid further criminal behaviour by understanding and changing the beliefs he may still have about the justifiability of violence and his presumed right to exercise authority over his partner. Unfortunately, much perpetrator counselling does not have these objectives. Instead, perpetrators are seen as people with low self-esteem, poor communication skills and, above all, poor anger management. These are then treated as the 'causes' to be tackled in counselling. The problem with the anger–management model is that it seeks to teach men to express their anger in non-violent ways, without necessarily questioning the justification for the anger in the first place. Thus, even a successful anger–management programme may simply substitute psychological for physical violence (Cox et al., 1989). Furthermore, like the conflict explanation of violence, the anger model ignores the fact that perpetrators seem quite capable of managing their anger in other situations—at work, for example. In short, much of the currently practised perpetrator counselling is thoroughly inappropriate as a response to domestic violence.

A final observation. Students of white-collar crime will find the argument we have been advancing strangely familiar. Domestic violence has been widely regarded as not really criminal, even though it is against the law. Similarly, offences by corporations and their executives against environmental, safety and commercial regulations have traditionally been regarded as falling short of criminal. Just as the women's movement has been arguing in recent years that crime in the home be treated as crime, so, too, academics and others have been been arguing in recent decades that white-collar crime is really crime and ought to be treated as such. In both cases there is a certain ambiguity in societal attitudes to the behaviour in question; in both cases offenders think of themselves as not real criminals. It is precisely the moral ambiguity of such behaviour which renders it particularly susceptible to shaming and thus prevention by the application of the criminal law.

10 Strategies for social change

There are two ways in which the explanation of social change can be approached. On the one hand it is possible to identify impersonal forces as the source of change; on the other, change can be seen as a product of human volition, as having been brought about by the conscious and intentional activity of human beings. Thus, for example, in seeking to explain the revolutions which occurred in Eastern Europe in 1989, one could point to the economic impasse in which the Soviet Union found itself in the 1980s which forced the progressive liberalisation of a number of aspects of Soviet life, in particular, its resolve to maintain its hold on the countries of Eastern Europe. On the other hand, one could attribute the changes of government to the extraordinary popular uprisings which forced the old regimes from power. This is a classic debate, known in social science writing as the structure–agency problem: is social change an outcome of changes in the social structure, over which individuals have little control, or is human agency responsible? One classic answer to this question was provided by Karl Marx (1977) when he wrote: 'men make their own history, but they do not make it just as they please; they do not make it under circumstances chosen by themselves, but under circumstances directly encountered, given, and transmitted from the past.'

Marx, in this passage, is acknowledging the role of both structure and agency, as do most attempts to deal with the problem, for clearly, there is an interaction between the two. Greig (1989), for example, has argued that if one wants to explain the occurrence of a revolution one must look to structural factors (economic circumstances, class structure etc.), to explain what made the revolution *possible,* and to human purpose and the activities and beliefs of the people involved, to understand why the revolution actually occurred and the direction it took.

One's position on the structure–agency issue vitally affects the way social movements are viewed. If impersonal forces are seen as the primary sources of change then social movements are the products of these forces and, at best, mediators of change. The questions which then suggest themselves for investigation concern the nature and identity of such movements, their class composition, the structural limits on their room to manoeuvre (Barbalet, 1989) and, of course, the material circumstances which brought them into existence (see Papadakis, 1989: 78). From this vantage point, the environment movement, for example, is viewed as having been generated by the escalating damage to the environment caused by unregulated processes of economic development.

If, on the other hand, human beings do make their own history, then social movements become sources of change in their own right and the tactics they adopt and the choices they make really do make a difference to outcomes. From this point of view, the analysis of movement strategies can contribute to an understanding of how social change is achieved.

The perspective emphasised here is that outcomes are not predetermined by large-scale social forces but are shaped in important ways by social movements and the strategies they adopt in particular circumstances. This perspective seems especially appropriate in the case of the movement against domestic violence. Unlike the environment movement which, it can be argued, was called into existence by mounting environmental destruction, the movement against domestic violence is not a response to any increase in the level of violence against women. Rather it is a by-product of the women's movement and the patriarchal analysis of society it produced. This view, incidentally, is supported by an American study which found that the existence of local feminist groups was a more important predictor of community programmes for battered women throughout the USA than per capita income, political liberalism or the existence of state domestic violence legislation (see Tierney, 1982: 211). The movement against domestic violence does seem to be a case of, in this instance, women making their own history.

The major aim of this chapter, then, is to reflect on the strategies used by the movement. We shall do so in the light of strategies used by other movements especially the environment movement.

THE STRATEGIES

The strategies used by the new social movements for social change (the peace, women's and environment movements) can be classified in many ways. The following is the most useful for present purposes. It is a modified version of a scheme used by Martin (1984) to discuss the strategies of the environment movement:

1 strategies aimed at grassroots change

2 strategies aimed at getting governments to act:
  (a) lobbying
  (b) electoralism
  (c) using the bureaucracy

This scheme is by no means clear cut in that many movement activities fall into more than one category. Furthermore, some strategies, such as the attempt by femocrats to change habits of thought and cultural practices within the public service itself, cut right across this classification. Nevertheless, social movement activities will often be found to rely on one of these strategies more than others. The basic distinction is between, on the one hand, grassroots methods, in which movement activists aim to bring about change by directly influencing the consciousness and behaviour of individuals, and on the other, methods which seek to persuade governments to implement change.

Grassroots methods

Grassroots methods aim to mobilise 'ordinary' people to become involved in processes of social change. Typically they involve forming new groups, or encouraging existing community groups, to discuss issues and to conduct educational activities (films, talks etc.). They also involve actions such as rallies, marches, letter writing campaigns and so on. The aim of these actions is not to pressure governments, although that may be a by-product, but rather to influence others in the community to consider the issue and to join the movement. Some of the otherwise seemingly irrational campaigns of some movements make sense when this purpose is borne in mind. For example, the anti-uranium movement's campaign to have local government areas declared nuclear-free makes little sense from a purely instrumental point of view, since most local governments have nothing to do with nuclear weapons or energy. But waging such a campaign raises awareness of the issue and stimulates the growth of the anti-nuclear movement more generally.

The best known grassroots tactic is the so-called 'direct action'. Attempts by peace activists to stage sit-ins in military bases, attempts by environmental protesters to stop logging by sitting in front of bulldozers and attempts by women to desegregate bars, again by staging sit-ins, are all examples of this form of action. It is 'direct' because it ostensibly aims to achieve movement objectives by directly obstructing the objectionable activity or practice: by forcing the abandonment of logging, by interfering with the operations of the base or by desegregating the bar by the very presence of the protesters.

Direct actions on a large enough scale can achieve movement objectives directly, as we have recently seen in Eastern Europe, where mass mobilisations made whole societies ungovernable. But, on the whole, they contribute to movement objectives more indirectly. They deepen the commitment of those involved; they raise awareness of the issue in the wider community and they may even apply pressure to politicians. Thus, direct action, although in some respects a grassroots tactic, is often also part of a strategy aimed at influencing governments.

The above examples of direct action involve civil disobedience, that is, violations of the law and confrontations with police. Protesters engaged in such actions are, in an important sense, taking the law into their own hands. There are other forms of direct action, however, which are not protests and do not involve confrontations with the state. Community organised environmental clean-up campaigns are a case in point. Movement activists see such campaigns as serving, not only the ostensible clean-up purpose, but also an educational and movement-building function (Malcolm, 1989).

A final feature of grassroots strategy is that it frequently involves an attempt to connect with the labour movement. As is pointed out in an excellent activist analysis of the campaign to save the Franklin River:

> ... the only way to change economic activity which causes environmental damage is to join with either capital or labour in the struggle over the shape of future investment strategies ... In the long term, unions are the more promising group for environmentalists to work with in their attempts to change Australian assumptions about 'good economics'. (Runciman et al., 1986: 94–5; see also Friends of the Earth, 1984: 16)

There is a history of attempts in Australia to form this connection, some successful, some less so. The green bans in Sydney in the early 1970s involved an alliance between local residents and the Builders Labourers Federation to prevent the destruction of residential neighbourhoods by developers. The anti-uranium movement, most active in Australia in the late 1970s, sought to involve waterside workers and other unionists in blocking the export of uranium. The environment movement has repeatedly, if sometimes belatedly, proposed methods of providing employment for people whose jobs are threatened by environmentalist demands. In the case of the movement against domestic violence, refuge workers have generally been strong unionists and have drawn on union resources to ensure levels of government funding sufficient to pay award wages. In this way the integration of refuge workers into the union movement has served to consolidate and to institutionalise their achievements.

Getting governments to act

There is a certain ideological dilemma involved in attempting to persuade governments to implement change since activists in the new social movements believe strongly in non-hierarchical, participatory forms of organisation and decision making (Pakulski, 1990). Nevertheless, it may at times be the only practical approach. One way of persuading governments to act is by lobbying, that is, by talking directly to decision makers in an attempt to convince or pressure them. The Women's Electoral Lobby is based on this strategy. Likewise, the Australian Conservation Foundation employs a liaison officer in Canberra whose primary function is to lobby politicians. Rational argument may sometimes win the day for lobbyists, but normally, to be effective, lobbying must be backed by clout of some sort—economic leverage in the case of business lobbying and electoral leverage in the case of the women's and environment movements. In the absence of such leverage, lobbying will be largely ineffective when other interests are at stake.

Electoral strategies can be of various sorts. A movement can publicise the position of all candidates on relevant issues and urge its supporters to vote for candidates, of whatever party, who support the movement's goals, as the Women's Electoral Lobby did in 1972. Or it can support one of the major parties, for instance the ALP, as the the Wilderness Society did in 1983 in its efforts to save the Franklin River. Or it can field candidates itself, either as independents, as the Greens have done in Tasmania, or as representatives of a new party, as the Nuclear Disarmament Party has done at various elections.

Electoral strategies frequently involve compromising movement goals. A recent example of this is the concession which the Tasmanian Green independents had to make to the Labor Party over areas to be listed for world heritage protection, as part of the price for achieving other objectives such as the abandonment of an environmentally destructive wood pulp mill project. Another objection voiced by movement activists is that electoral strategies tend to disempower supporters by transferring power away from the grassroots to elected leaders. This may ultimately undermine the whole movement. Furthermore, from a practical point of view, after an exhausting electoral campaign, particularly if it is seen as unsuccessful, the movement may temporarily disintegrate (Martin, 1984: 111).

As far as the use of bureaucratic apparatuses is concerned, in the case of the environment movement state environmental protection agencies have made some contribution to movement goals. Such agencies have, however, been entirely dependent for their impact on governmental resolve and thus ultimately on the political impact of the wider movement. An agency established by the Hawke government in 1989 in an attempt to reconcile the conflict between environmentalists and industries exploiting natural resources, the Resource Assessment Commission, may also turn out to be a bureaucratic agent of the environment movement, provided environmentalists manage to put their arguments effectively to the Commission.

In the case of the women's movement, bureaucratic agencies have been much involved in promoting womens issues, most notably the various offices of women's affairs at state and federal levels. Likewise, equal employment opportunity tribunals have contributed significantly to the advancement of women's interests (Grabosky, 1989).

Any social movement uses a mixture of the strategies discussed above. The questions which we can now address are these. What mix have movements in fact used to gain momentum? Can we draw any conclusions about why particular mixtures have been adopted? For comparative purposes we shall consider first the strategies used in the campaign to save the Franklin River, before reconsidering the movement against domestic violence.

THE FRANKLIN CAMPAIGN

In the early 1980s environmentalists took on the Tasmanian government and that state's Hydro-electric Commission (HEC) in an attempt to stop the damming of the Gordon River, which would also have flooded the Franklin (see Runciman et al., 1986; Martin, 1984). The strategies used were primarily aimed at governments, first the Tasmanian and later, the federal. The Tasmanian Wilderness Society, which spearheaded the campaign, concentrated initially on lobbying politicians and on community education, using glossy publications and films to convey the beauty of the wild rivers, and bringing in celebrities to gain media attention. The aim was to generate a climate of public opinion which would persuade the Tasmanian Labor government to reject the HEC proposals. The government, however, believed firmly in the policy of 'hydro-industrialisation' as a way of promoting economic growth, and despite mounting public opinion against the HEC proposals, and a division within its own ranks, was not prepared to concede to the environmentalists. Dissident Labor MPs eventually brought down the government, and at the ensuing election the Liberal Party gained office. But the Liberals were also pro-dam. Thus, the parliamentary strategy in Tasmania had failed.

The Tasmanian Widerness Society (TWS) now transferred its attention to the mainland and, in conjunction with mainland groups, began a campaign to get the federal Liberal government to intervene, which after some agonising, it refused to do. As a result, in November 1983, conservation groups announced that they would support the ALP and the Democrats at the next federal election. This they did with great skill and vigour, targetting particular marginal seats most likely to be influenced by their campaigning. By this stage, then, the movement had adopted a conventional electoral strategy in the hope of having a government elected which was sympathetic to its aims.

Meanwhile, TWS had for some time been planning to take direct action to blockade construction work when it actually began. In December 1982 work started on the access roads and the blockade swung into action. This was certainly a grassroots action in which activists from all over Australia participated. The campaign involved obstructing the transportation of bulldozers into the area as well as the road construction work itself. It was essentially a civil disobedience campaign in which, all told, over 1000 protesters were arrested. But the blockaders could not hope to seriously impede construction work. The blockade was first and foremost a media event, carefully stage managed, with organisers briefing journalists and providing numerous opportunities for dramatic television footage of confrontations between protesters and police. In reality, the blockade was aimed at mainland television audiences and in this it was highly successful: the public was treated nightly to scenes of the beautiful Tasmanian wilderness and of the dramatic attempts by blockaders to save it. Perhaps the most powerful media images to come out of the campaign were the flotillas of inflatable dinghies challenging barges bringing bulldozers up the Gordon River.

The timing of these events could not have been more favourable for environmentalists, since the blockade occurred in the lead up to the federal election of March 1983. The ALP won and it was widely perceived that the campaign to save the Franklin, and in particular the electoral tactics adopted, had swung the election (but see Warhurst, 1983). The new government immediately moved to prevent further construction work and the Tasmanian government appealed to the High Court on the grounds that the federal government did not have the constitutional power to intervene. The court eventually decided, four votes to three, in favour of the federal government. So, finally, the conservationists were victorious.

The campaign to save the Franklin was not aimed at changing the thinking or behaviour of individuals in relation to the environment generally. It did not seek to change people's consumption habits in the interests of achieving more sustainable, less environmentally destructive life styles. It was not, in short, seeking grassroots change. Rather, it aimed to get governments to act on a particular conservation issue. Thus the strategies used were all directed at governments rather than at ordinary people. Of course, ordinary people were important in that they had to be persuaded to vote for a particular party, but the aim was to have change imposed from the top rather than building social change from the bottom up.

Despite its success, the campaign to save the Franklin has drawn considerable criticism from environmental acitivists concerned about building a longer-term movement for change. According to Martin (1984: 117):

> ... by adopting electoral methods, the anti-dam movement drained its own strength, undercut cross-party support (by alienating Liberal voting conservationists), disempowered its supporters, and put the fate of the dam in the hands of the High Court in which public opinion and activist commitment play little role ... The entire issue in the end hinged on one person—the swinging High Court judge—thus symbolising the pyramidal structure of the 'appeal-to-elites' approach.

Martin concedes that where a movement is concerned to achieve an urgent short-term goal, such as stopping a dam, it may be appropriate to focus on governments. But significant social change is unlikely to occur, he argues, so long as a movement remains fixated on 'urgent threats', necessitating immediate government action. Such an approach fails to address the need for change in values and behaviour at the individual level. To use a favourite movement slogan, it fails to acknowledge that 'the personal is political'. Major social change will only occur, he concludes, when movements focus on grassroots mobilisation.

While Martin's position is a coherent one in principle, the fact is that the environment movement is built, quite naturally, on a series of 'urgent threats' requiring governmental action: the hole in the ozone layer, massive tanker oil spills, the logging of the planet's rapidly diminishing virgin rain forests, the pollution of beaches by sewage and so on. Furthermore, Martin probably underestimates the extent to which the environment movement, in fighting such issues, is slowly influencing individual attitudes and behaviour. The growth of paper recycling is one example of grassroots change which has perhaps been generated by a focus on urgent threats. Whether this process will lead to more fundamental shifts in consumption patterns, only time will tell. Interestingly, the social change model which Martin advocates seems more applicable to the movement against domestic violence, as we shall see in what follows.

THE MOVEMENT AGAINST DOMESTIC VIOLENCE

The movement against domestic violence has adopted grassroots strategies to a greater extent than the environment movement. Essentially what it sought was not a government decision on the issue, but a change in the consciousness and behaviour of men and women throughout the society. Change was therefore to be achieved primarily through grassroots activity, with government playing a secondary, though nonetheless indispensible role in the whole process.

Concern about domestic violence grew out of the grassroots consciousness-raising processes of the broader women's movement and culminated in action by groups of women around the country to establish refuges. This was very much a direct action approach to social change. In the case of the first women's refuge in Sydney the action also involved civil disobedience, since in order to establish the refuge a group of women simply occupied vacant housing in defiance of the law. The aim of this direct action was somewhat different from the blockades of the environment movement, which do not really expect physically to prevent environmental destruction and are primarily aimed at putting pressure on governments. In contrast, the women involved in the establishment of refuges, as well as aiming to focus public attention on the issue, really did expect to provide direct relief to the victims of male violence.

Clearly, domestic violence cannot be eliminated by government decision. Nevertheless, there were certain decisions which governments could take to facilitate the efforts of refuge workers to bring about change. Most obviously, they could fund the refuges. They could also reform the law to enable the courts to protect victims more effectively. Finally, they could fund new initiatives taken by the movement such as the DVCS in Canberra. None of this involved handing over responsibility to governments to bring about change; government action would simply facilitate what was essentially a grassroots process.

What, then, have been the strategies used by the movement to get governments to act supportively? First, lobbying has clearly been one, although seldom carried out with the professionalism of the environment movement. Second, electoralism has not been a favoured strategy. Domestic violence has never been an explicit electoral issue, and the movement against domestic violence has neither stood its own candidates nor endorsed those of another party. Indeed, with the exception of the 1972 election, when the Women's Electoral Lobby rated all candidates on their attitudes on women's issues, the women's movement as a whole has not relied on electoral strategies to advance the cause of women. It has, of course, exerted a certain amount of electoral pressure, in the sense that politicians have been generally concerned to attract the women's vote and so have often been sympathetic to women's issues. But the cross-party nature of the women's movement has tended to preclude the use of electoral strategies.

Working through bureaucratic agencies has, however, been a central strategy of the movement against domestic violence. State and federal governments all have women's units of various kinds advising on women's issues and, as we have seen, the femocrats who staff these units have played important roles in promoting outcomes favourable to the movement. Femocrats promoted refuge funding requests inside government, while in the specific case investigated in this study, the establishment of the DVCS in Canberra, femocrats entered into an active partnership with refuge workers to bring about the required change.

Finally, we should note that some of the strategies adopted by the movement against domestic violence fall outside the categorisation we have been using. The educational campaign conducted by the OSW amounted to an attempt by government to bring about grassroots change. Such a strategy would seem quite paradoxical to some social movement activists.

We see, then, that the mix of strategies employed by the movement against domestic violence has been very different from the mix in evidence in the campaign to save the Franklin. Why the difference? To a large extent it is a function of the issues. As we pointed out at some length in chapter 1, domestic violence is located in the private sphere, not the public arena. It cannot, therefore, be eliminated simply by government decision; what is required is a fundamental change in the way men regard and relate to women. It was natural, therefore, for the movement against domestic violence to focus its energies at the grassroots or community level. On the other hand, the plan to dam the Franklin, realistically, could only be defeated by government decision. It was predictable that the Franklin campaign would be aimed at influencing governments.

Another conclusion suggested by the comparison we have been making is that, regardless of the mix of strategies employed, direct action plays a crucial role, either as part of a grassroots strategy, or as part of an attempt to influence electorates via media coverage.

In both cases it is those engaging in direct action who are the spearhead of change. The commitment and courage of these activists is a vital part of the process. Without protesters confronting bulldozers or sitting high in trees defying police efforts to dislodge them, many environmental issues would never make it onto the political agenda. Without the refuge workers' commitment to the cause of battered women, the movement against domestic violence would not have made the progress it has.

There is one other observation still to be made about the movement against domestic violence. While it has clearly been an outgrowth of the women's movement and is still driven by that movement, various other groups and interests have taken up the issue in such a way as to broaden the movement beyond its feminist base. The view of domestic violence taken by these groups has often been quite distinct from and at times even in conflict with the feminist analysis of the type outlined in chapter 9. We saw, for instance, in our discussion of the origins of the DVCS in Canberra, that marriage counsellors, law reform agencies and politicians all played significant roles. None of these groups was motivated by explicit feminist concerns. It has also been noted that many of the refuges around Australia are run by religious groups and other organisations not part of the women's movement. Finally, the press, in taking up the issue as it has from time to time, has tended to treat it in a way that is inconsistent with a feminist analysis. Wife batterers have been seen as monsters, beasts, exceptional men, quite unlike the great majority of men. Feminist analysis has stressed, in contrast, that such behaviour is not the behaviour of abnormal men and is an expression of deep-seated patriarchal values. In short, the movement against domestic violence encompasses more than just the women's movement, even though the latter remains its inspiration.

THE FUTURE OF THE MOVEMENT AGAINST DOMESTIC VIOLENCE

The likely fate of movements such as the movement against domestic violence is clearly a matter of importance. Two contrasting possibilities have been suggested: either they become co-opted, largely as a result of reliance on government funding, and lose their character as movements for change; or the organisations and institutions created by the movement become permanent features of a changed social landscape and themselves agents of further change.

It has been argued that the battered women movement in the USA which has been very much a grassroots phenomenon, as in

142 WORKING FOR CHANGE

Australia, in time will be taken over by government (Tierney, 1982: 216–17). It will be 'tamed' by its reliance on government funding (see also Studer, 1984: 420). Refuges will increasingly be staffed by 'professionals' and operate with a conventional social service orientation rather than a feminist vision. The movement will be steered away from its feminist critique of the patriarchal nature of society and its demands for radical social change. Furthermore, because the growth of the battered women movement in the USA has depended in part on media attention, the inevitable decline in media interest will sap the movement of its influence.

The alternative possibility is suggested by Spector and Kituse (1973) in what they call a four-stage natural history model of social problems. In the first stage, groups assert the existence and offensiveness of some condition. This generates, secondly, some response from official agencies. Thirdly, this response is found to be inadequate by the complainant groups who, fourthly, take matters into their own hands by creating alternative or parallel institutions to deal with the problem. Examples of such new institutions would be: alternative newspapers, food co-ops, single-issue political parties and so on. They argue that these developments represent significant social change. While the details of this model do not appear to fit the emergence of the domestic violence problem in Australia, the authors' conclusion that the process results in significant change does describe the Australian situation rather better than the co-optation model described above, as we shall suggest in what follows.

The movement against domestic violence in Australia has resulted in the creation of a series of new organisations, notably the many refuges around the country, and more recently a number of crisis services, such as the Canberra DVCS. The refuges, in particular, are community based, and many, but not all, are run by feminist collectives. Possibly because of the mediation of a sympathetic femocracy, the feminist refuges have been able to resist the pressure to become conventional social service deliverers, despite receiving government funds, and have persisted with their aim of empowering women and undermining patriarchal practices. Indeed, as we argued in our discussion of the refuge movement, they have even managed to sharpen their social change focus. The process of institutionalisation which the movement has undergone has thus strengthened rather than weakened it.

Furthermore, while the media have played a role in Australia in promoting domestic violence awareness, the progress of the movement has not depended on media interest, as is the case, according to Tierney (1982: 217), in the USA. Indeed, it is perhaps a measure of the lack of media coverage that the federal government decided to launch its advertising campaign in 1989.

We have seen that the continuing progress of the movement against domestic violence in Australia is in part attributable to the femocrat phenomenon. The engagement of the women's movement with the state has gone further in Australia than in other countries and there is no doubt that this has played a part in the sustaining the momentum.

But what is also apparent is that the progress of the movement in Australia has depended more than anything else on an interactive partnership between grassroots workers and femocrats and, despite the stresses and strains inherent in this partnership, it remains a creative force. It is this cooperation, rather than the efforts of any one group, that has been the basis of the movement's success.

Finally, the organisations established by the movement against domestic violence, and in particular the DVCS, are stimulating further change in their interaction with agencies such as the police and the courts. We explored in detail in earlier chapters the way in which the DVCS has impacted on the legal system, confronting it with a feminist analysis of domestic violence and winning some small measure of support for this analysis, at least among higher level functionaries. The very organisations which the movement fought to establish have now become agents of change in their own right.

The achievements in the area of domestic violence have interesting implications for speculation about the broader women's movement in Australia. The view is widespread that the impact of feminism is waning. Here is one recent statement of the position:

> Government initiatives for women are important in tackling inequality, but the women's movement itself has lost momentum. It does not have the grassroots strength it had at the outset of the century when women were campaigning for the vote, or the strength it in had in the late 1960s and early 1970s when the women's liberation movement proved itself to be a force to be reckoned with. (Waller, *The Canberra Times* 8 March 1990)

Certainly it is true that the women's movement is no longer novel or particularly newsworthy. But it is not clear how one might justify the claim that it has lost momentum. In the particular case of domestic violence the women's movement has been very active throughout the 1980s and, as we have seen, grassroots activism has been a vital part of the process. In this area at least, women's liberation is still a force to be reckoned with.

References

AFP (Australian Federal Police), no date, *Domestic Violence: Notes for the Guidance of Police Officers*

Anderson, J. and C. Dean (1989) 'Renaming rape: a social reality reframing survival: a feminist practice model', paper available from CASA House 270 Cardigan St Carlton 3083

Australian Housing Research Council (1980) *Women in Last Resort Housing,* Department of Housing and Construction

Barbalet, J. (1989) 'Social movements and the state: the case of the American labour movement', in C. Jennett and R. Stewart (eds) *Politics of the Future: The Role of Social Movements* Melbourne: Macmillan

Barrios de Chungara, Domitila (1978) *Let Me Speak* New York: Monthly Review Press

Berk, R.A. and P.J. Newton (1985) 'Does arrest really deter wife battery?' *American Sociological Review* 50 (2) 253–62

Beryl—Canberra Women's Refuge, *Annual Reports*

Bograd, M. (1990) 'Why we need gender to understand human violence' *Journal of Interpersonal Violence* 5(1), 132–5

Braithwaite, J. (1989) *Crime, Shame and Reintegration* Melbourne: Cambridge University Press

Braithwaite, J. and G. Geis (1982) 'On theory and action for corporate crime control' *Crime and Delinquency* (April), pp. 292–314

Brett, Waller and Williams (1989) *Criminal Law 6th ed.* Sydney: Butterworths

Brooks, S. (1986) 'The role and functions of the Office of the Status of Women and Government Achievements', unpublished paper available from OSW, Dept. of Prime Minister and Cabinet

Brownmiller, S. (1975) *Against Our Will: Men, Women and Rape* Harmondsworth: Penguin

Chambers, B. and J. Pettman (1986) *Anti-Racism Handbook* Canberra: AGPS

Connell, R.W. (1987) *Gender and Power* Sydney: Allen and Unwin

Cox, J., S. Holt, S. Lazarus, K. McCarthy (1989) 'Domestic violence', unpublished paper delivered at Australian Law and Society conference

Curthoys, A. (1984) 'The women's movement and social justice', in Broom (ed.) *Unfinished Business* Sydney: George Allen and Unwin

Daly, M. (1978) *Gyn/Ecology: The Meta-Ethics of Radical Feminism* London: The Women's Press

Daniels, K. and M. Murnane (eds) (1989) *Australian Women: A Documentary History* Brisbane: Universitiy of Queensland Press

Dixson, M. (1986) 'Gender, class and the women's movements in Australia 1890, 1980', in N. Grieve and A. Burns (eds) *Australian Women: New Feminist Perspectives* Melbourne: Oxford

Dobash, R.P. and R.E. Dobash (1981) 'Community response to violence against wives: charivan, abstract justice and patriarchy' *Social Problems* 28(5), 563–81

——(1979) *Violence Against Wives: A Case Against Patriarchy* New York: Free Press

Dowse, S. (1984) 'The bureaucrat as usurer', in Dorothy Broom (ed.) *Unfinished Business* Sydney: George Allen and Unwin.

——(1981) 'The transfer of the Office of Women's Affairs', in Sol Encel et al. (eds) *Decisions: Case Studies in Australian Public Policy* Melbourne: Longman Cheshire

——(1983) 'The women's movement's fandango with the state', in Cora Baldock and Bettina Cass (eds) *Women, Social Welfare and the State* Sydney: George Allen and Unwin

——(1989) 'A great swell in the tide' *Australian Society* (October), pp.8–9

Dunford, F, D. Huizinga and D. Elliot (1990) 'The role of arrest in domestic assault: the Omaha police experiment' *Criminology* 28(2), 183–206

Eccles, S. (1984) 'Women in the Australian labour force', in D. Broom (ed.) *Unfinished Business* Sydney: George Allen and Unwin

Edwards, S. (1985) 'Male violence against women: excusatory and explanatory ideologies in law and society', chap. 9 in S. Edwards (ed.) *Gender, Sex and the Law* London: Croom Helm

Elliot and Shanahan Research (1988) *Summary of Background Research for the Development of a Campaign Against Domestic Violence* Available from OSW

Feldman, S. (1986) *Second Thoughts: A Review of the Past, Present and Future of Victorian Women's Refuges* unpublished WESP evaluation

Fisse, B. and J. Braithwaite (1983) *The Impact of Publicity on Corporate Offenders* Albany: State University of New York

Ford, Prudence (1988) *Homes Away for Home—SAAP Review,*

Vol II: Sub-program Evaluations—Women's Emergency Services Program

Fox, R. and A. Freiberg (1985) *Sentencing: State and Federal Law in Victoria* Melbourne: Oxford

Franzway, S. (1986) 'With problems of their own: femocrats and the welfare state' *Australian Feminist Studies* 3 (Summer), pp.45–57

Franzway, S., D. Court and R.W. Connell (1989) *Staking a Claim: Feminism, Bureaucracy and the State* Sydney: Allen and Unwin.

Freeman, J. (1973) 'The tyranny of structurelessness' *Ms* July, pp.76–8, 86–9

Freeman, J. (1983) *Social Movements of the 60s and 70s* New York: Longman

Friedan, B. (1963) *The Feminine Mystique* New York: Norton

Friends of the Earth (1984) *Strategy Against Nuclear Power* Canberra: unpublished pamphlet

Girdler, Maria (1982) 'Domestic violence: social solutions', in Carol O'Donnell and Jan Craney (eds) *Family Violence in Australia* Melbourne: Longman Cheshire

Goode, M. (1985) 'Drugs, alcohol and the law' *Australian Alcohol and Drug Review* 4, pp.217–23

Greig, A. (1989) *States, Parties and Revolutions* PhD thesis, Australian National University

Grabosky, P. (1989) 'Sex discrimination: Wardley v Ansett', in P. Grabosky and A. Sutton (eds) *Stains on a White Collar* Sydney: The Federation Press

Hatty, S. (ed.) (1986) *National Conference on Domestic Violence: Proceedings* Canberra: Australian Institute of Criminology

——(1987) 'The criminalisation of women battery: an apparent alliance between feminists and the state' *New Zealand Social Work Journal* 12, 1 and 2, pp.6–11.

——(1988) *Male Violence and the Police: An Australian Experience* Sydney: School of Social Work, University of NSW

Hazlehurst, K. (1989) 'Violence, disputes and their resolution', paper prepared for the National Committee on Violence, available from the Australian Institute of Criminology

Homel, R. (1990) 'Crime on the roads: drinking and driving', in J. Vernon (ed.) *Alcohol and Crime* Canberra: Australian Insititute of Criminology

Hopkins, A. (1981) 'Class bias in the criminal law' *Contemporary Crises* 5, pp. 385–94

Jaffe, P. et al. (1986) 'The impact of police charges in incidents of wife abuse' *Journal of Family Violence* 1,1, 37–49

Jenkins, A. (1990) *Invitations to Responsibility* Adelaide: Dulwich Centre

Johnson, Vivien (1981) *The Last Resort: A Women's Refuge* Melbourne: Penguin

Kelly, P. (1989) *The Domestic Violence Crisis Service Inc.: Evaluation 1988-1989* (unpublished)

Kirby, M.D. (1980) 'Reforming the law', in A. Tay and E. Kamenka (eds) *Law Making in Australia* Melbourne: Longman Cheshire

Knight, R.A. and S. Hatty (1988) 'Violence against women in Australia's capital city' *Victimology*

Law Reform Commission—Australia (1986) *Domestic Violence* Report No.30 Canberra: AGPS

Lawson, O. (ed.) (1990) *The First Voice of Australian Feminism: Excerpts from Louisa Lawson's The Dawn 1888-1895* Brookvale, New South Wales: Simon & Schuster

McFerren, L. (1987) *Beyond the Image* A review of WESP in Western Australia

——(1990a) 'Interpretation of a frontline state: Australian women's refuges and the state', in S. Watson (ed.) *Playing the State* Sydney: Allen and Unwin

McGregor, H. (1990a) 'Conceptualising male violence against female partners: political implications of therapeutic responses' *ANZ Journal of Family Therapy* 11,2, pp. 65-70

——(1990b) 'Domestic violence: alcohol and other distractions' in J. Vernon (ed.) *Alcohol and Crime* Canberra: Australian Institute of Criminology

McNeely, R. and C. Richey Mann (1990) 'Domestic violence is a human issue' *Journal of Interpersonal Violence* 5(1), 129-32

Malcolm, S. (1989) *Local Action for a Better Environment* Self-published PO Box 452 Ringwood, Vic. 3134

Martin, B. (1984) 'Environmentalism and electoralism' *The Ecologist,* 14, 3, pp.110-18

Marx, K. (1977) 'The eighteenth brumaire of Louis Bonaparte' in *Selected Writings* edited by D. McLellan, Oxford Univ. Press, p.300

Mercer, J. (ed.) (1975) *The Other Half* Ringwood: Penguin

Millet, K. (1970) *Sexual Politics* New York: Doubleday

Morehead, A. and R. Penman (1989) 'Federal government information campaigns: a critical review', occassional paper no.11, Communication Research Institute of Australia, Canberra

Morgan, R. (1989) *The Demon Lover: On the Sexuality of Terrorism* London: Methuen

Mugford, J. (1989) 'Domestic Violence', paper available from the Australian Institute of Criminology, Canberra

National Committee on Violence (1990) *Violence: Directions for Australia* Canberra: Australian Institute of Criminology

New South Wales Task Force on Domestic Violence (1981) *Report*

New South Wales Domestic Violence Committee (1985) *Report* Sydney: Women's Coordination Unit

New South Wales Women's Advisory Council (1987) *A Decade of Change: Women in NSW 1976–86* Sydney: Women's Coordination Unit

Nieuwenhuysen, J. and J. Hicks (1975) 'Equal pay for women in Australia and New Zealand', in B. Pettman (ed.) *Equal Pay for Women* Bradford, UK: MCB Books

O'Donnell, J. and J. Craney (eds) (1980) *Family Violence in Australia* Melbourne: Longman Cheshire

O'Donnell C. and H. Saville (1980) 'Sex, class inequality and domestic violence', in J. Scutt (ed.) *Violence in the Family* Canberra: Australian Institute of Criminology

——(1982) 'Domestic violence and sex and class inequality', in C. O'Donnell and J. Craney (eds) *Family Violence in Australia* Melbourne: Longman Cheshire

OSW (Office of the Status of Women) (1988) *Community Attitudes towards Domestic Violence in Australia* (available from OSW)

Pakulski, J. (1990) *Social Movements: The Politics of Moral Protest* Sydney: Longman Cheshire

Papadakis, E. (1989) 'Struggles for social change: the Green Party in West Germany', in C. Jennett and R. Stewart (eds) *Politics of the Future: The role of social movements* Melbourne: Macmillan

Patterson, A. (1980) 'Crisis intervention', in J.A. Scutt (ed.) *Violence in the Family* Canberra: Australian Institute of Criminology

Pizzey, E. (1974) *Scream Quietly or the Neighbours Will Hear* London: Penguin

Pringle, R. and A. Game (1976) 'Labour in power: the feminist response' *Arena* 41, 71–78

Queensland Domestic Violence Task Force (1988) *Report: Beyond These Walls*

Randall, M. (1980) *TodosEstamos Despiertas: Testimonios de la Mujer Nicaraguense Hoy* Mexico: Siglo Veintiuno

Reid, Elizabeth (1987) 'The child of our movement: a movement of women', in J. Scutt (ed.) *Different Lives* Melbourne: Penguin

Ronalds, C. (1990) 'Government action against employment discrimination', in S. Watson (ed.) *Playing the State* Sydney: Allen and Unwin

Ross, S. (1982) *The Politics of Law Reform* Melbourne: Pelican

Rossi, L. (1989) 'Contribution' in Anna Maria Khan-Guidi and Elizabeth Weiss (eds) *Give Me Strength—Forza e coraggio: Italian Australian Women Speak* Broadway, NSW: Women's Redress Press

Runciman, C., H. Barber, L. Parlane, G. Shaw and J. Stone (1986)

Effective Action for Social Change: The Campaign to Save the Franklin River Melbourne: Victorian Environment Centre

Ryan, L. (1990) 'Feminism and the federal bureaucracy 1972–83', in S. Watson (ed.) *Playing the State* Sydney: Allen and Unwin

Saville, Heather (1982) 'Refuges: a new beginning to the struggle', in O'Donnell and J. Craney (eds) *Family Violence in Australia* Melbourne: Longman Cheshire

Sawer, M. (1989) 'Pressure without power' *Australian Society,* (October), pp.46–7

——(1990) *Sisters in Suits* Sydney: Allen and Unwin

Sawer, M. and M. Simms (1984) *A Woman's Place: Women and Politics in Australia* Sydney: George Allen and Unwin.

Schwartz, R. and S. Orleans (1967) 'On legal sanctions' *University of Chicago Law Review,* 34, pp.274–300

Scutt, J. (1979) 'Woman Bashing: The Failure in Police Response' in *Proceedings of the National Conference of Women's Advisors, New South Wales'* Department of the Premier, Sydney, NSW; also in O'Donnell and Craney, 1980; revised version published as 'Invading Private Lives. The Police Response to Woman Bashing' in *2nd Women and Labour Conference Papers* 1980, Radical Publications, Melbourne

——(ed.) (1980) *Violence in the Family* Canberra: Australian Institute of Criminology

——(1982) 'Domestic violence: the police response', in C. O'Donnell and J. Craney (eds) (1980) *Family Violence in Australia* Melbourne: Longman Cheshire

——(1983) *Even in the Best of Homes* Melbourne: Penguin

——(1985) 'United or divided? Women inside and women outside against male lawmakers in Australia' *Women's Studies International Forum* 8(1), pp.15–23

——(1986) 'Women, reform and the law' *Australian society* (April), pp. 24–28

——(1986) 'Going backwards: law reform and women bashing' *Women's Studies International Forum* 9(1), pp. 49–55

——(1988) 'The privatisation of justice: power differentials, inequality, and the palliative of counselling and mediation' *Women's Studies Forum* 11(3), pp. 503–20

——(1990) 'Violence and sexual politics' a paper presented in Adelaide on 23 April to the National Training Forum

Scutt, J. and D. Graham, (1984) *For Richer, For Poorer–Money, Marriage and Property Rights* Ringwood: Penguin

Seddon, N. (1986) 'Legal responses to domestic violence–what is appropriate?' *Australian Quarterly* 58(1) 48–59.

——(1989) *Domestic Violence in Australia: The Legal Response* Sydney: The Federation Press

Sharp, R. and R. Broomhill (1990) 'Women and government budgets' *Australian Journal of Social Issues* 25 (1), 1–13

Sherman, L. and R. Berk (1984) 'The specific deterrent effects of arrest for domestic assault' *American Sociological Review* 49 (April), 261–72

Smith, A. (1985) 'Women's refuges: the only resort?' *Public Private* pp.23–68

Spector, M. and J. Kituse (1973) 'Social problems: a reformulation' *Social Problems* 21, 145–59

Stratmann, P. (1982) 'Domestic violence: the legal responses', chap. 7 in C. O'Donnell and J. Craney (eds) *Family Violence in Australia* Melbourne: Longman Cheshire

Studer, M. (1984) 'Wife beating as a social problem: the process of definition' *International Journal of Women's Studies* 7(5), Nov/Dec, 412–22

Summers, A. (1986) 'Mandarins or missionaries: women in the federal bureaucracy' in N. Grieve and A. Burns (eds) *Australian Women: New Feminist Perspectives* Melbourne: Oxford

Thomas, D. (1970) *Principles of Sentencing* London: Heinemann

Tierney, K. (1982) 'The battered women movement and the creation of the wife beating problem' *Social Problems* 29(3): 208–20

Wallace, A. (1986) *Homicide: The Social Reality* Sydney: NSW Bureau of Crime Statistics and Research

Walker, N. (1985) *Sentencing: Theory, Law and Practice* London: Butterworths

Ward, E. (1985) *Father–Daughter Rape* New York: Grove

Warhurst, J. (1983) 'Single-issue politics: The impact of conservation and anti-abortion groups' *Current Affairs Bulletin* 16, 2 (July), pp. 19–31

Wearing, R. (1989) 'Domestic violence: the importance of local knowledge' *Arena* 87, 47–52

Weatherburn, D. (1990) 'Sources of confusion in the alcohol/crime debate' in J. Vernon (ed.) *Alcohol and Crime* Canberra: Australian Institute of Criminology

Wills, S. (1983) 'The women's liberation movement', in R. Lucy (ed.) *The Pieces of Politics, Third Edition* Melbourne: Macmillan

Yeatman, A. (1990) *Bureaucrats, Technocrats and Femocrats* Sydney: Allen and Unwin

Younger, Barbara (1986) 'Domestic violence: ideology and practice', in S. Hatty (ed.) *Domestic Violence,* Proceedings of a Conference, Australian Institute of Criminology, Canberra